Routledge Revivals

Modern Production Among Backward Peoples

First published in 1935, *Modern Production Among Backward Peoples* (now with a new foreword by Barbara Ingham) stands as a groundbreaking early contribution to development economics. In this pioneering work, the author challenges prevailing colonial assumptions about indigenous economic systems, rejecting the conventional wisdom that labelled tropical populations as "primitive". Instead, she presents a sophisticated analysis of labour dynamics in plantation economies and smallholdings across colonial territories.

The author integrates political economy, classical theory, and institutional perspectives to demonstrate how labour supply responded to complex historical, social, and legal influences rather than inherent cultural limitations. Her examination of tropical development within the context of European colonial expansion offers remarkable perspectives that remain relevant to contemporary discussions of economic inequality and development. This book is a must-read for researchers of development economics and economic history to understand the intellectual foundations of their fields.

Modern Production Among Backward Peoples

I.C. Greaves

Routledge
Taylor & Francis Group
Routledge Revivals

First published in 1935
by George Allen & Unwin Ltd

This edition first published in 2025 by Routledge
4 Park Square, Milton Park, Abingdon, Oxon, OX14 4RN

and by Routledge
605 Third Avenue, New York, NY 10158

Routledge is an imprint of the Taylor & Francis Group, an informa business

Publisher's Note
The publisher has gone to great lengths to ensure the quality of this reprint but points out that some imperfections in the original copies may be apparent.

Disclaimer
The publisher has made every effort to trace copyright holders and welcomes correspondence from those they have been unable to contact.

A Library of Congress record exists under LCCN: 35013272

ISBN: 978-1-041-15314-6 (hbk)
ISBN: 978-1-003-67884-7 (ebk)
ISBN: 978-1-041-15322-1 (pbk)

Book DOI 10.4324/9781003678847

Modern Production
among
Backward Peoples

by

I. C. Greaves
M. A. McGill, Ph.D.(Econ.) London

London
George Allen & Unwin Ltd
Museum Street

FIRST PUBLISHED IN 1935

Thesis approved for the degree of Doctor of Philosophy in the University of London. And published with the aid of a grant from the Publication Fund of the University

PRINTED IN GREAT BRITAIN BY
UNWIN BROTHERS LTD., WOKING

Foreword to the Reissue

Ida Greaves' *Modern Production among Backward Peoples* (1935) is a remarkable pioneer study in the discipline of development economics, focusing on labour supply in plantations and peasant smallholdings in tropical areas, under a variety of social, political and legal influences. Sadly, it has been much neglected. Routledge's current reissue of the book as an economics classic is to be warmly welcomed. It will introduce a new generation of readers to one of the most illuminating treatises of early development literature.

Ida Greaves was born in Barbados in 1907 and educated in economics and political science at McGill University in Canada, at a time when the economics department was under the leadership of Stephen Leacock. Leacock was a complex character, best known as a humourist writer, but also a theorist of the American institutionalist school, having studied with distinction under Thorstein Veblen at Chicago. Ida Greaves' 1935 book, reissued here, shadows institutionalist thinking, focusing less on the immutable laws of the market, and more on human motivations as they change and mature under the influence of different social, political and legal histories.

After graduating from McGill, Ida Greaves held research and teaching fellowships at Radcliffe College (Harvard) and Bryn Mawr College in the United States. In 1932 she applied for admission to the London School of Economics and was accepted as a PhD (Econ) student. Alongside her academic work she connected in London with many of the leading feminist activists of the day. *Modern Production among Backward Peoples* is based on the doctoral thesis she produced at the London School of Economics between 1932 and 1934. The thesis itself was described as 'brilliant' by the three distinguished professors who were her examiners at doctoral level. It was they who recommended it to the publishers, George Allen and Unwin. It was published in 1935 in the Series *Studies in Economics and Commerce*. So, the question for the present-day reader is whether the book is indeed a neglected classic, one which has remained in obscurity. Thanks to this reissue, today's readers will have the opportunity to decide on its merits for themselves.

An obvious reason why the book failed to secure a place in the economics literature is that it appeared in print at a difficult time. Though it was reviewed in major journals on publication, academic life in Britain would shortly be severely disrupted by preparations for war. Indeed, when the book was published, Ida Greaves herself had already left London for her home in Barbados. Her Studentship at LSE had come to an end in 1934 and she had no independent financial resources. She was in no position to publicise her work in London, or to capitalise on the success of her doctoral research at the London School of Economics.

There is also the problematic issue of the book's title, with its reference to *backward* peoples. Many potential readers may have been dissuaded over time from exploring the contents of a book with such an outmoded title. In the 1950s and 1960s when development economics had come of age, underdeveloped or developing had replaced terms such as primitive or backward. Those adjectives were regarded as shameful, or even racist. Some potential readers may even have concluded that the book was only of ethnographic or antiquarian interest.

Nothing could be further from the truth. The book's title had been selected by the publishers and not by Ida Greaves. It was wholly misleading. The reader who took the trouble to go beyond its title would have discovered that the book presented instead a rare and outspoken *critique* of the way in which populations in tropical areas were assumed by economists to be primitive and backward. The standard textbook approach as epitomised in Marshall's *Principles,* was that indigenous peoples were "*governed by the fancy of the moment*", subject to custom and impulse, and incapable of taking the long view. This was the very approach which Ida Greaves set out to demolish.

In 1972, almost forty years after the publication of Ida Greaves' book, George Beckford of the University of the West Indies, Mona, Jamaica, published his own pioneering study of underdevelopment in the plantation economies of the world. It offered an interpretation of underdevelopment which stressed the need for an understanding of the institutional environment in which individuals operated. Economics alone could not explain the process of development. There was a need for political economy to reassert itself. Beckford, the acknowledged leader of the radical "plantation school" of social scientists, cited the influence of Ida Greaves' early work, pointing out her contribution in relating human behaviour in a plantation economy to the export of metropolitan enterprise and capital. Beckford uniquely recognised the path-breaking contribution of *Modern Production among Backward Peoples.* It set tropical development firmly within the historical experience of European colonial expansion. Ida Greaves' analysis of labour supply in her 1935 book is remarkably thorough and thought provoking. It does not evade the difficult issues of the 1930s but bravely tackles the malign influences on labour supply arising from three centuries of European expansion.

Ida Greaves' idiosyncratic blend of classical political economy, history and institutional factors was probably not the orthodox treatment to be expected from an economist at the London School of Economics. There was no school of thought to which it could be readily assigned, and no group of colleagues pursuing similar ideas. This may go far in explaining its failure to take any hold in the development economics of the 1950s and 1960s. It invites comparison with the widespread popularity of the Lewis model, with its single supply schedule for labour covering all historical and institutional cases.

Ida Greaves, who died in London in 1993, is best remembered now for her work on the colonial currency boards. Her views on the advantages of the colonial currency system attracted a strong negative response from economists at the time, though she always defended her corner robustly. More recently in the work of economists such as Anna Schwartz and Steve Hanke, her analysis of the workings of the colonial currency boards has received much praise. The reissue of her 1935 book may encourage further reappraisal of the contribution of Ida Greaves as a pioneer female development economist.

Barbara Ingham, June 2025

Author of *Ida Greaves, A Pioneer Development Economist*,
Routledge, Taylor and Francis Group,
New York and London, 2024

PREFACE

For modern civilization backward peoples take the place that barbarians had in the ancient world. But while the aims of that world ended with conquest, the aims of the modern world begin there, for at the present time trade is the most obtrusive form of triumph. The *Jus Gentium* of to-day is the law of economics, and the equity functions of the *Praetor Peregrinus* are discharged in the commodity markets.

It is a natural correlative of this situation that the governments of overseas dependencies should pay increasing attention to problems of production. There are special Departments in the territories of all the Powers for the improvement and regulation of production, and special provision in many for subsidizing it as well. In contrast with this, it might be said that one characteristic of Dominion status is full responsibility for the conditions of internal industry. And in the cause of progress the Dominions have set about achieving a state of self-sufficiency, while in the cause of civilization the Imperial Government is abolishing that state which it found in the dependencies. It is, however, only with the latter conditions that the investigation in this book is concerned. It is an analysis of the economic metamorphosis that accompanies the extension of imperial rule over hitherto remote and self-sufficing communities. And hence its inquiry is confined to the conditions that constitute change. The question of whether there ought to be such change, or of what changes would be better, is entirely beyond its scope. And it is indeed fortunate to be able to escape the difficulty of explaining why barter between two tribes in Africa is deplorable backwardness which must be improved, while barter between two nations in Europe is a step forward in the methodology of civilization and to be encouraged.

The abundant literature on the subject has, however, dealt almost exclusively with its cultural aspects, and the present investigation has not had the benefit of any substantial precedents or models from the standpoint of economic analysis. Not only is primitive economy a field that the economist has largely ignored, but some of the contributions from other sources have treated it as the graveyard of economics. To reproduce all the assertions which science as well as sentiment in the sphere of backward society appears to have regarded as a lethal blow to economic theory would be both tedious and futile. Instead, I have endeavoured to subsume these societies under the same analytical technique as is applicable to those more advanced. And I hope that the relationship between the two, and the nature of the transition that is required of the backward, have been made clear enough to dispel such misapprehensions as to their essential and irreconcilable differences as are usually claimed to have an economic basis.

The survey of modern production has been based on contemporary agriculture in the tropics. It ought not to be necessary to point out that tropical products do not conform precisely to the geographical delimitation of these regions. In some places altitude offsets the effect of latitude, and in others rainfall is too low to produce the effect that might be expected of the temperature. One example of the variation of crop distribution will illustrate the effect of such climatic differences. The South-East of the United States has long been one of the most important cotton-producing areas, although cotton is a crop that grows practically everywhere in the tropics. On the other hand, although the best habitat of coffee is at the temperate altitudes of tropical areas, it has never been cultivated in the United States, in spite of this country being the largest consumer of the product. The reason for choosing agriculture as a basis instead of mining, which is sometimes regarded as the dominant type of modern production in backward regions, is that the latter industry is a wholly foreign enterprise imposed on indigenous economy, and not a stage of continuous internal development. Furthermore, probably because the foreign interests represented in mining have been well recognized, it is already the subject of an extensive literature, whereas agriculture has been relatively neglected. But if the plantation is an historical form of production, the peasant may well be called a prehistoric one; and the agricultural producer is of primary importance in the process of capitalization that is transforming primitive economy. If a stable exchange economy is to be established, the comparative costs of production of the plantation and the peasant is a matter of first importance. Under conditions of political freedom these costs will be practically the sole determinant of the course production will take. And even where complete freedom of choice does not exist, a proper estimate of cost conditions would seem to be necessary to a successful policy of regulating production.

Since the designation "native" has been used with a variety of connotations from the avowedly political to the obscurely scientific, it may prevent misunderstanding to state that the term is used here merely to describe the indigenous inhabitant of a particular area, and carries no qualitative implications.

It is obvious that the subject of investigation has bordered —in some opinions it may have trespassed—on many different fields of learning and particular departments of knowledge, and a bibliography that contained all possible references would be prohibitively extensive. It has been my object therefore to append in bibliographical form only such works as contain direct reference to forms of production, or the productive activities, of people conventionally comprised in the title category. Where similar publications of different dates are available, I have chosen the most recent I found. Where I have made use of particular information from other sources I hope it has been adequately acknowledged in the footnotes. But to find an individual citation for some of the more general opinions to which I have occasionally referred would be to discriminate unwarrantably between a large class of supporters.

The book was written while I held the Woman's Studentship at the London School of Economics, and I am glad to have this chance of thanking the donor and committee for the opportunity of undertaking the investigation. To Professor Plant I am indebted for much generous attention and stimulating discussion; but to attribute responsibility to him on that account for all the views that follow would be unjust.

The Library of the Royal Empire Society was an exhaustive and incomparable source of material, and I am extremely grateful for the unfailing assistance I received there. At the Libraries of the Imperial Institute and the Colonial Office I also obtained useful information on various occasions.

I. C. GREAVES

CONTENTS

ABBREVIATIONS

D.O.T.: Department of Overseas Trade Report.
E.C.G.R.: Empire Cotton Growing Review.
E.M.B.: Empire Marketing Board.
I.C.I.: Institut Colonial International.
I.L.O.: International Labour Office.
I.L.R.: International Labour Review.
I.Y.A.S.: International Yearbook of Agricultural Statistics.
J.A.S.: Journal of the African Society.
J.T.A.: Journal of Tropical Agriculture.
Y.C.C.D.: Yearbook of Compared Colonial Documentation.

MODERN PRODUCTION AMONG BACKWARD PEOPLES

CHAPTER I

THE DEMAND FOR PRODUCTS FROM THE TROPICS

FROM the earliest times the natural products of the tropics have been of importance in international trade. They were carried over the caravan routes from the East, they formed the cargoes of the first merchant ships on the Mediterranean, and they were sold in the markets of the Hansa. It was the wealth of distant tropical lands that stimulated the activity of the Age of Discovery, and it lies at the basis of modern imperialism.

In the course of this long trading history both the volume and the variety of tropical products have steadily expanded, and their place and significance in international trade have undergone important changes. The things most wanted in the first place were the "Spices of the Indies"—pepper, cloves, cinnamon, and ginger—which were not only a valuable addition to the coarse food of the time, and the only means of preserving fresh meat then known,[1] but were also regarded as possessing remarkable medicinal properties.[2] Other exotic goods which became highly valued additions to the narrow

[1] "Medieval men had neither a delicate palate nor the means of gratifying it with choice meats; their meat was coarse and they liked it highly flavoured. Spices, therefore, played a large part in medieval cookery and were bought in prodigious quantities for the kitchens of the great—the spicery bill for the royal household in the twenty-ninth year of Edward I being close on £1,600." L. F. Salzman, *English Trade in the Middle Ages*, p. 420.

[2] H. S. Redgrove, *Spices and Condiments*, traces the history of the medicinal qualities of ginger, p. 32; cinnamon, p. 92; cloves, p. 137; pepper, p. 174.

range of European products were the handicrafts of the East—muslins from Calicut, brass from Benares, silks and porcelain from Cathay[1]—all of which helped to build the legend of the fabulous wealth of the Indies that dominated the commercial enterprise of Western Europe for over a century. From America the Spanish drained the precious metals that circulated from Flanders to China, while the Dutch and the English sought in the East to control the sources which had fed the Arab trade routes and Venetian markets, sources which the Portuguese had first discovered by sea but failed to hold. The Tudor monarchy in England raised commercial "adventuring" to the highest level of national aspiration, and a new school of political philosophy taught that "there is much more to be gained by Manufacture than Husbandry, and by Merchandise than Manufacture."[2]

Spices were a peculiarly appropriate commodity for risky ventures in the small ships of the sixteenth century. Their value was high in proportion to their storage space, the demand for them was comparatively inelastic so that prices could be maintained by a monopoly, and the profits on voyages that succeeded amply compensated for the losses on those that failed.[3] But both the volume and the value of

[1] A Portuguese carrack captured in 1592 by some of the earliest English adventurers carried 8,500 quintals of pepper, 900 of cloves, 700 of cinnamon, 500 of cochineal, and 450 of porcelain, silks, musk, amber, and precious stones. The total value was £140,000. C. E. Fayle, *A Short History of the World's Shipping Industry*, p. 129.

[2] Sir William Petty, *Political Arithmetick*.

[3] A. G. Keller, *Colonisation*, p. 420, states that on nutmegs the Dutch made a profit of as much as 5,000 per cent, and cloves purchased at 4 stivers per pound in the Bandas sold at 4 guilders per pound in Amsterdam. When the Dutch had the monopoly of pepper in London in the 1590's they raised the price from 6s. to 8s. per pound, but in 1603 four ships of the East India Company's first voyage returned to England with full ladings, and a sharp slump in the pepper market ensued. The Lord Treasurer was at the same time trying to sell a cargo of captured pepper on behalf of the King, and refused to let the Company

the spices were in the long run overshadowed by the varied trade that grew along the routes they had opened up. Sugar, indigo, cotton, coffee, and tea proved the substance of a larger and more valuable trade than nutmegs, cloves, and ginger, and even gold and silver, had ever been. It is significant that the Spaniards should now be remembered more for the empire they destroyed in the Andes than for that they established across the Atlantic.

By the end of the seventeenth century some commodities of tropical origin, such as sugar and tea, which had first been regarded as curiosities and luxuries in Europe, were accepted as necessary foodstuffs, and others such as tobacco and rum were equally desirable. In the production of all of these European capital had been increasingly invested, and when the indigenous population of the West Indies and the American colonies proved insufficient it was supplemented by imported slaves from Africa—who represented a further capital investment. Thus the early trading connection between Europe and the tropics developed permanent investment interests which have ever since been a dominant influence in the progress of those regions. The European colonies in Louisiana, Virginia, and the Carolinas were originally founded to export sugar, cotton, and tobacco, but the growth of population in North America made that continent into an importer of tropical products, and was an important factor in the increased demand for coffee, cacao, sugar, oilseeds, and hemp in the nineteenth century.

The expansion of manufactures in Europe in the eighteenth and nineteenth centuries gave rise to a new type of demand for tropical commodities. Hitherto these had been required almost entirely for final consumption, but now they

offer theirs on the market, so it was divided among subscribers to the venture at 2s. per pound, but the selling price fell to 1s. 2d., and still stocks remained unsold. Sir William Foster, *England's Quest of Eastern Trade*, p. 7.

acquired additional importance as the raw material of several large industries. Coconut oil for soap and margarine; palm oil for tin-plate rolling, confectionery, and candles; palm kernel oil for margarine and confectionery; jute for sacks; Manila, Mauritius, and sisal hemp for cordage and canvas; and rubber, indispensable accessory of motor transport, all come entirely from the tropics, along with a large proportion of the world's cotton. Moreover, products such as sugar, cacao, and tobacco, which were originally imported for consumption only, are now used in industrial countries for manufactures which are exported to other non-producing areas, and sometimes to the producing ones also. Tropical products[1] are no longer the isolated con-

[1] An indication of the relative importance of these in international trade is given in *Plantation Crops*, E.M.B./C/5, 1932. "The value of international trade in sugar and coffee is exceeded only by the trade in raw cotton and wheat, on the basis of average values in the years 1926–31, and the world's trade in rubber, tea, or tobacco, on the same basis, is greater than that in beef or pork, maize or barley." But the acreage under export crops in the tropics is small compared with that

(*Exports in Million Cwts.*)

CROP	1909–13	1928–30	PERCENTAGE INCREASE 1928–30 OVER 1909–13
RICE	90	125	39
SUGAR*	143	244	71
CACAO	4·5	10·1	124
TEA	6·7	8·2	22
COFFEE	21	28·6	36
GROUNDNUTS	10·8	31·2	189
COPRA	10·8	22·3	106
PALM OIL	2·4	4·9	100
PALM KERNELS ..	6·3	10·9	73
JUTE	15·5	16·1	4
RUBBER	1·8	14·7	717
BANANAS	24	46	92
SESAMUM	5·3	2·8	Decrease 47

* Includes beet sugar.

[*Footnote continued on p. 23*

tribution to international trade which they were when the Portuguese bargained at the Court of the Moghul, but an integral part of the world's industrial system.

The exports from the tropics at the present time can conveniently be divided into five classes:

1. Staple articles of consumption and important raw materials.
2. Spices.
3. Drugs.
4. Dyes, gums, and lesser industrial products.
5. Fruit and minor foodstuffs.

I.[1] *(In Millions of Quintals)*

CROP	PRODUCTION	NET EXPORTS
CACAO	5·7	4·9
COCONUTS*	—	2·0
COCONUT OIL*	—	2·7
COPRA*	—	10·5
COFFEE	16·0	15·4
COTTON	56·3	27·6
GROUNDNUTS†	53·4	16·3
JUTE	20·4	6·5
MANILA HEMP	2·0	—
PALM OIL AND KERNEL OIL* ..	—	2·8
PALM KERNELS*	—	5·7
RICE†	921·0	63·0
RUBBER	—	8·5
SUGAR (cane)	173·8	118·8
TEA*	—	4·0

[1] Figures from *I.Y.A.S.* for the harvest year of 1930.
* No accurate returns of production in many areas.
† Production partly estimated.

under the staple food crops of either temperate or tropical countries (p. 5). The same survey points out the impossibility of obtaining accurate figures of production and acreage for most of the tropics; practically complete statistics of trade, however, are available. Subject to some reservations as to completeness and precision, *World Agriculture*, 1933, gives the figures of recent trend in trade of tropical products.

2.[1] SPICES have lost their early pre-eminence in tropical trade to products with more extensive industrial uses, and have to some extent been displaced for food-flavouring purposes by synthetic condiments; but if the place they hold in commerce is now small, nevertheless the services they render to consumption are still important. PEPPER is the largest export in this class and amounts to about 800,000 hundredweight annually; CAPSICUMS are shipped from several regions, along with CHILLIES from India, CARDAMONS from the East Indies and Ceylon, and GRAINS OF PARADISE from West Africa. GINGER exports, including the preserved product from Canton, are over 230,000 hundredweight; and ALLSPICE or PIMENTO, a product peculiar to Jamaica, amounts to about 50,000 hundredweight. Ceylon exports 45,000 hundredweight of CINNAMON, and a similar bark, CASSIA, is shipped from other parts of the East. CLOVES amount to about 180,000 hundredweight, and NUTMEGS to 125,000, while MACE is available to about 20 per cent of the latter. VANILLA, which is cultivated chiefly by the French, amounts to 15,000 hundredweight.

3. DRUGS. Products with specific medicinal properties were for the most part recognized and used by the people of their indigenous habitat before they were discovered by Europeans, and for some of them, e.g. ARECA NUT and CASTOR OIL, local consumption is still more important than exports. CINCHONA, the bark which yields quinine, is the outstanding example of a drug cultivated for export by Europeans; and others which have a place of some importance in pharmacy are ALOES, BALSAM OF PERU—which comes from El Salvador; COCA, from which cocaine is made; IPECACUANHA, LIGNUM VITAE, and SARSAPARILLA.

[1] Figures from *Plantation Crops*, cit. supra. Annual yields are often affected by weather conditions, but over the last ten years there has been no change in the trend of production. H. S. Redgrove, *Spices and Condiments*, 1933.

4. DYES, GUMS, and lesser industrial products. Until very recently vegetable pigments were the only kind of dyes available, and they grew almost entirely in tropical regions. For general industrial purposes natural dyes have been almost entirely replaced now by chemical synthetic products, although the former are still used for the fine colouring of many Oriental handicrafts, and for much of the morocco leather prepared at Kano. Distinctive dyes which are still exported to some extent are ACACIA, ANNATTO, CAMWOOD, COCHINEAL, FUSTIC, INDIGO, and LOGWOOD. TURMERIC is still used both as a spice and a dye; and GAMBIER and QUEBRACHO are important tanning materials. GUM ARABIC has increased in use with synthetic dyes as the base of fabric printing processes; and COPAL and SHELLAC are in widespread demand as varnishes. BALATA and GUTTA-PERCHA are latex products from tropical trees somewhat similar to rubber, but of less tensility, and the former is used largely for machine belting. The TAGUA, or VEGETABLE IVORY, NUT holds a very specialized place in commerce, and so does PIASSAVA FIBRE, which is similar to whale bone when dried. KAPOK, the silky fibre of the ceiba tree, has become increasingly popular as a stuffing for pillows and upholstery. By-products from some staple commodities have also attained some measure of industrial importance, the chief example being OILCAKE for cattle feed from the residue of vegetable oils; and more recently such by-products of sugar-cane as insulating material made of bagasse, power alcohol, and solid carbon dioxide, have been attracting attention.

5. FRUITS and minor foodstuffs. One of the most spectacular developments in tropical exports in recent years has been provided by BANANAS. This, as well as the export trade in PINEAPPLES and CITRUS FRUITS, has been made possible by the provision of cheap refrigerated transport. The greater part of citrus fruit exports, however, still comes from sub-

tropical countries, but the banana is wholly a tropical product, and attempts are being made to add the MANGO to the regular supplies in foreign markets. ARROWROOT, TAPIOCA, and SAGO are tuber products with definite, if limited, uses; and YERBA MATE is a leaf of the forests of Paraguay and Brazil which yields a beverage similar to tea. KOLA NUTS and SHEA NUTS are exported to a small extent, but are more used for internal consumption; while the latex CHICLE of the sapodilla tree has acquired its importance wholly from the popularity of chewing-gum.

The extensive development of tropical production which these exports reveal could not proceed without a profound effect upon the territories involved. In the beginning it was the new supplies from the tropics which exerted a powerful influence upon European economy, but since the seventeenth century the forces of change have been reversed, and it is the demands of Europe and America which have been transforming the customary economy of the tropics. It has become usual in recent years to describe the inhabitants of this geographical belt as "backward peoples" because they have not kept pace with the mechanical development of Western civilization. These are lands in which the climate did not stimulate man to energetic effort, survival was possible at a low level of subsistence, and the Industrial Revolution was brought to them from outside. The great commercial cities of Europe in the Middle Ages confined their interests in foreign lands to trade and business, they did not accompany their ventures by the machinery of political control. Indeed, their efforts had usually to be directed to securing their own freedom from political interference at home. But since the sixteenth century the growth of trade between Europe and the tropics has been accompanied by the extension of European power over all territories that appeared to be of economic importance; and under differing degrees of political control the greater part of the tropical belt now forms part of the empire of European civilization.

It is only in Abyssinia, Siam, and the south of China that an indigenous people still retains both the traditional form of its internal economy and the control of its foreign relations. Liberia is ruled by Americanized negroes, and for the natives independence of the white race does not mean freedom from its methods. The Republics of Central America were founded as colonies of Spain, and Brazil as a colony of Portugal, and their subsequent rise to independence has made the indigenous population subservient to the aims of Iberian culture. The trend of economic development in these countries bears, in consequence, a marked resemblance to that in areas which are still under imperial government.

The British established trading-posts in India and acquired colonies in the West Indies early in the seventeenth century when imperialism in its modern form of maritime expansion was beginning; afterwards they extended their rule to Ceylon, Mauritius, and Malaya, and numerous islands in the Pacific; and most recently to large areas of West, East, and Central Africa. The Dutch established an East Indies trading company earlier than the British, and eventually took over the government of islands sixty-five times the size of Holland. The French were also early in the West Indies and India and after losing their foothold in the latter acquired Indo-China, and rule besides Madagascar, an extensive area in West Africa and several islands in the Pacific. In spite of her early colonial enterprise Portugal retains now only two territories in Africa and some small areas in Indonesia; and Porto Rico and the Philippines, which the wars of Europe had left to Spain, became territories of the United States after the war between these two countries in 1898. Belgium has inherited the Congo Free State established by King

Leopold; and Australia assumed imperial responsibilities with the Protectorate of New Guinea in 1906, while New Zealand acquired mandates in the Pacific in 1919.

Except for the early settlements in the West Indies, imperial relations with tropical territories did not take the form of colonization in the classical meaning of the term. It was not population that went out from the Mother Country to establish new colonies, but commercial interests which made contacts with new areas and then endeavoured to bring the indigenous population under the imperial flag. The territories that were in origin real colonies have now become Republics or Dominions, and the tropical empires of European nations consist almost entirely of annexed areas with their native peoples, who are being either trained or compelled to serve the ends of civilization. A French theorist pointed out some years ago that France really had no colonies but only dominions, since her empire consisted not of French emigrants but of alien "dominated" races;[1] and the same criticism would apply to what is called the colonial empire of other Powers. But since the British countries which were really colonies have chosen the status of Dominion to indicate their attainment of political freedom from the Mother Country, the use of the term for places now governed by imperial domination is hardly feasible.[2] In some parts of the tropics which are of sufficient altitude to enjoy an almost temperate climate, e.g. Southern Rhodesia, Kenya, and Katanga, an effort has been made to settle white communities on the land. But besides being few, these have had only a limited success. On the other hand the coffee industry of the Santo Paulo plateau in Brazil, like that of the cool highlands of Costa Rica and Colombia, has been developed entirely by immigrants from the South of Europe.

[1] Jules Harmand, *Domination et Colonisation*, 1909.

[2] A. G. Keller, *Colonisation*, 1908, discusses fully types of colonies and colonization, pp. 1–20.

As far as modern colonial areas are concerned, however, the development of the tropics by European capital has followed a system of cultivation distinct from one of colonization, and this has meant that the native labour supply has always been a factor of supreme importance. "It is a modern riddle of the sphinx," says Keller, "at which the various nations have guessed, each in its characteristic way."[1]

The earliest method of obtaining products from the tropics was that of primitive barter, when coloured beads and bright calicoes and hand mirrors, as well as rum and gin, were exchanged for ivory or gold dust or slaves. But in some places not even these cheap "trade goods" were offered, and the imperial Power exacted supplies of local commodities by a process of direct extortion. No productive contribution was made by the foreign agent, and it was by this method that the Dutch East India Company brought Java to a state of collapse, and King Leopold exhausted the people and products of the Congo Free State. In other places there were no local organizations through which the imperial Power could exert pressure, and when the required crops had to be cultivated they could only be obtained by introducing a plantation system. The Government granted large areas to investors, either individual or corporate, and they then had to secure labourers to do the work of cultivation. It was the early demand for plantation labour of this sort that led to slavery and the slave trade, and since they were abolished various methods of inducing or coercing natives to work have been devised; or alternatively, a supply of immigrants has had to be obtained. It became apparent as the foreign demand for tropical products increased that it was not sufficient for an imperial Government to keep its colonies out of the control of rival Powers, but that it should at the same time either take an active part in developing the natural resources of the colonies or encourage

[1] A. G. Keller, *Colonisation*, 1908, p. 580.

foreign entrepreneurs to do so. Then followed a phase of imposed development which sought to adjust production in tropical areas to the requirements of international conditions. The natives were compelled either to work for foreign employers or to grow a saleable surplus over their consumption needs, and this is the situation over a large area at the present time. But with increasing experience it became apparent that the same principle of development could be followed by making the natives into producers and traders on their own account, and schemes for training the indigenous cultivators to grow export crops on their own land have been instituted with marked success in the British West African Protectorates, in Uganda, in the Belgian Congo, and in the Netherlands East Indies.

But while these two opposite methods of production are the subject of controversy in some circles, they are not at present to be differentiated by any single geographical or political principle. In some places, and under different metropolitan Governments, as in Java and Malaya, the two are found side by side. The French have administered West Africa on the basis of native farming, but Equatorial Africa on the basis of foreign concessions. The British have developed Nigeria and the Gold Coast entirely through native production, but in Kenya native interests are subordinated to European farming. There is, besides, in both native and plantation cultivation a wide range of variety in the size of units, in the degree of capitalization, and in the organization of labour. Nor has either system a definitive policy of cultivation. The planting of a revenue crop by Africans tends to substitute individual for tribal tenure, and fixed cultivation for shifting. But in the forests of Central America Europeans grow bananas and cocoa by the same shifting methods which they condemn as wasteful in Africans at home. In some territories both food for local consumption and export crops are grown by plantations as well as native farmers, while in others production is entirely for sale, and foodstuffs have to be imported. Thus the Nigeria and Uganda cotton farmers are also self-supporting, and the Cameroons plantations grow food for their labourers, but the groundnut farmer in Gambia depends on imported rice, as do the plantation labourers of Ceylon, Malaya, and Mauritius.

In conclusion it might be said that at the present time the State which exercises control over a backward territory expects to perform three functions: to maintain the supply of exports from the territory, to protect the profitability of foreign investments in the territory, and to develop among the natives a market for its own manufactured exports. Were the metropolitan power aiming merely at obtaining a large volume of raw materials as cheaply as possible—as Spain did in America and the Dutch at first in the Indies, it could exact compulsory labour at the lowest cost compatible with the continuity of the supply. But in establishing a market for imported goods it is clearly desirable to expand local purchasing power at the same time, and the goal of development is then not to keep the native standard of living as low as possible by depressing the price of labour, but to make the exchange value of native labour as high as possible by increasing its efficiency.

Assurances from official sources that the metropolitan powers have recognized the need of raising instead of exploiting the subsistence level are becoming frequent, although in some territories adequate machinery for implementing it still appears to be lacking. It was not until a late date in imperial history that the existence of well-defined social systems in colonial areas and their significance for new cultural contacts was recognized. Before that they were ignored and sometimes destroyed. But in the course of the last half-century this attitude has undergone a radical change, and the importance of indigenous institutions to the introduction of new methods of economic development is widely, if not universally, recognized. The British have refused any concessions which would conflict with the rights of native tribes in their West African Protectorates; the Dutch have purchased for restoration to native use land previously granted to foreigners; the French promise security of tenure to their African subjects who register title to their land; and in most territories the initially immense foreign concessions have been drastically reduced. The official international attitude to "Backward Peoples" has also been authoritatively re-defined. Instead of being the assets of conquerors they are now the wards of civilization, and their lands and natural resources are held in trust by the imperial Power, to be administered to the mutual benefit of native owner and foreign consumer.

Abstract considerations alone, however, do not determine policy, and what appears to be a uniform theory shows in practice a wide diversity of regional adaptation. The execution of a scheme of colonization is in the first place subject to the influence of geographical and climatic factors. In some places mountains and forests presented effective barriers to conquest by the limited mechanical resources of earlier centuries, and rights of trade and penetration had to be secured by a form of treaty with the local chiefs. There were also areas which the nature of the climate marked off as unsuitable for European settlement, and which could only be developed through the natives. These were the conditions, for instance, that guided official policy and formed the basis of native agriculture in British West Africa, whereas the sub-tropical plateau of East Africa which was attractive to European settlers has been responsible for an entirely different native policy in that part of the continent. The next determining factor is the state and number of the indigenous population. The first simple assumption that all primitive people were the same did not stand empirical test.

Some races, notably in the East, were highly organized politically; and after showing itself resistant to foreign forces of disintegration, their customary organization provided stable units of government through which the metropolitan power could exercise control. The native communities of Indo-China and Malaya, for example, have retained their vitality in spite of being absorbed into the currents of imperialism, but the aborigines of the West Indies were rapidly exterminated by the same influences. And not the least important factor in the differentiation of policy is the national character of the metropolitan country and the nature of the political system which it regards as embodying law and civilization. All the imperial powers have now eloquently recognized their mission to civilize the savage, but a survey of the territories they rule gives the impression that neither in law nor practice is the civilization homogeneous.

Behind all formulations of policy there is, however, the same cause. The insufficiency of indigenous labour in some places, and its reluctance in others, has presented obstacles to foreign development ever since European capitalism became aware of the natural resources of the tropics; and the primary problem of tropical production remains in the twentieth century as it was in the seventeenth, the problem of an adequate labour supply. In the succeeding chapters we shall examine the methods by which the interest and effort of the native of the tropics has been directed to meeting the demand for products from his land.

CHAPTER II

INDIGENOUS ECONOMY AND FOREIGN CAPITALISM

THE indigenous systems of economy found in the tropics comprise a wide variety of types in which the economic unit may be either the family, the clan, the village community, the feudal fief, or the tribe; and their forms of political organization vary from the simple uniformity of all members of the community, and the disparate equalitarianism of more diversified skill and occupations, to the distinctly complex stage of a functional hierarchy. The contemporary range of agrarian systems includes forest cultures which are little more than the gathering of wild products, and garden culture round the family dwelling, as well as the regular cropping of more distant village and tribal land. Similarly, the methods of production range from the digging-stick of the women in West Africa to the cattle-drawn plough of India, and include the improvident shifting cultivation of Negroes and Moros as well as the diligently tended rice terraces of Java. But although they are all clearly differentiated from the structure and conditions of European industrialism, it is not possible to define any one type as representative of tropical economy as a whole; this includes both different types, and the same type at different stages of development, and in the opinion of one agricultural expert presents at the present time "an epitome of the various stages of evolution through which the art has passed in all places, these stages often lying side by side in the same country."[1]

These are the types of society which are described indiscriminately as backward, primitive, and even savage, in comparison with modern European civilization; and before examining the contacts between them it might be well to

[1] C. A. Barber, *Tropical Agricultural Research in the Empire*, E.M.B., 2.

consider the exact implications of this terminology of comparison. "Backward" as a description of a different or a subject people is a distinctly modern term. The old civilizations used "barbarian" or "alien" for the purpose, which seems to mean that their measure of superiority connoted a different qualitative basis of comparison from ours. What are the criteria of backwardness? When is a society primitive —must the classification distinguish between a rudimentary stage of progress and elementary methods of living that have become permanent? Is the savage to be identified by nudity of body or by blankness of mind? Is pigmentation a better guide to cultural status than more intangible qualities? Or is it power that is the measure of the superiority of the new civilization of Europe over the old civilizations of the tropics? The attempts at classification which might have answered these questions are not entirely convincing. If the "trouble with the savage is that he has no hypothetical attitude to truth," then Europe is still enjoying a rich legacy of savagery. Thurnwald describes the primitive races as having "lived always in the peripheral regions of human culture,"[1] but it would be interesting to know why they did; and, moreover, the periphery of culture cannot be said to exclude some who are regarded as backward to-day. According to the Covenant of the League the backward races are those "unable to stand alone under the strenuous conditions of modern life," and this is the situation of subordinate minorities in Europe as well as subordinate majorities in Africa, and if they were left alone they would not find the conditions of life so strenuous. As for the criterion "the savage's understanding of elementary economic principles is very limited,"[2] this would exclude many leading social reformers from the ranks of civilization.

[1] R. H. Thurnwald, *Economics in Primitive Communities*, p. 279.

[2] E. E. Muntz, "The Early Development of Economic Concepts," *Economic History*, No. 1, 1926.

But if it is difficult to distinguish the civilization of Europe from that of the tropics in matters of principle, no such difficulty is found if more concrete methods and practices are taken as the standard of comparison. The two types of society are clearly identifiable by their respective economic systems; and it is in these that the essential contrast between backwardness and advancement is to be found. The philosophy of the English artisan and the French farmer may or may not be better than that of the Haussa craftsman and the Malay peasant, but their productivity is greater, and their standard of living can therefore be higher. Only a few hundred years ago the Orient was in the eyes of Europe a place of fabulous wealth, it had accumulated through centuries riches that Western countries had scarcely known for as many years; yet India and China are to-day poverty-stricken in comparison with these same countries. It is with the character of this recent European development and its difference from the long static continuity of the Orient and Africa that we are here concerned.

Contrary to the early expectations of Europeans it soon became apparent that heathen had a civilization, and scientific investigation revealed that even savages had a culture, but very little attention was paid to their economic organization as such. For one thing the political economists of the nineteenth century were fully occupied with the phenomena of their own countries; for another, the savage had been removed from the sphere of realistic discussion by becoming the unhistorical ideal of utopian speculation; and so, noble and indolent, he provided a useful—and unsubstantiated—antithesis to the economic man. "Whatever be their climate and whatever their ancestry," said Marshall, "we find savages living under the dominion of custom and impulse; scarcely ever striking out new lines for themselves; never forecasting the distant future; fitful in spite of their servitude to custom, governed by the fancy of the moment; ready at times for the most arduous exertions, but incapable of keeping themselves long to steady work. Laborious and tedious tasks are avoided as far as possible; those which are inevitable are done by the compulsory labour of women."[1] And because he regarded them as possessing all these unregenerate qualities, the opposite in every respect of contemporary German Kameralism, Bücher relegated savages to a pre-economic state of society.[2] But such a method is as invalid as it is unnecessary. "Economics is concerned with mankind in the ordinary business of life," whether the business is conducted in a furskin or a frock coat, or without them. Except in a few Biblical instances, humanity has not obtained sustenance without effort; and the relation of the means to the ends of living which this effort represents is the substance of economic analysis. Means and ends vary in different places at the present time, and have varied in the same place at different times; and while it is not admissible to judge one economy by the standards of valuation of another, this does not mean that separate frameworks of theory have to be devised for them.

Thurnwald introduces his study of *Economics in Primitive Communities* by saying, "I think we have to construct several homines oeconomicos, each representing the economic tendency of one type, or even of one stratum within it." But he ends with the conclusion, "If we are to regard the fundamentals of primitive economics with a balanced and realistic mind we are struck by the fact that we see the same emotional powers at work as with us, only sometimes in different proportions."[3] If this is true, then homo oeconomicus is essentially the same in every type of society, and

[1] *Principles of Economics*, 8th edition, Appendix A.

[2] *Industrial Evolution*, 1900, p. 12. And in 1926 Max Schmidt, in *The Primitive Races of Mankind*, follows Bücher's theory to the conclusion that "there are two chief forms of production—the communal and the economic." P. 176.

[3] Op. cit., p. 278.

to treat him as varying in character because the concrete manifestations of his impulses and satisfactions differ in time and place is to invite a needless confusion of thought. It is the function of fulfilling wants, not the phenomena of fulfilment, that is an economic concept. In Africa hunting is usually a means of obtaining food, in Europe it is sometimes an end in choosing an occupation; but this difference in the method of obtaining satisfaction cannot be taken to indicate different motives in the economic subjects. That it probably is evidence of different ethical and aesthetic standards merely means that economic analysis does not discriminate between the ends which society pursues, and homo oeconomicus is the same in Zimbabwe and Bengal as in New York. Economic theory has for the most part dealt with man in the modern commercial economy because it is in this complexity of relationships, where competing scales of valuation determine the ends that shall be served and many alternative means are available for use, that there is most need of economic analysis; and it is no doubt a consequence of this concentration of attention that economic activities have come to be identified with the pecuniary calculus of motivation familiar under modern conditions. Once this assumption is made, then some other classification has to be found for those societies that carry on their work under different conditions of production and distribution. But as Marshall pointed out, while "some parts of the modern analysis of distribution and exchange are inapplicable to a primitive community," it is not true that "there are no important parts of it which are applicable."

In the foregoing quotations the term "primitive" is used as a convenient contrast with Western industrialism, and it applies in this sense not only to the tropics at the present time but to the pre-industrial ages of the countries that are now economically advanced. We must therefore consider the characteristics that distinguish these two categories of human achievement. As we saw above, the societies that are generally classed as primitive comprise a wide range of economic systems, differing considerably in their organization and methods of production, but they are all differentiated from modern industrial economy by a few fundamental conditions from which the multiplicity of more superficial differences result. These conditions are a different quantitative relationship between the factors of production, land, labour, and capital. It is true that the particular usage of any people or locality has been dictated to a great extent by those peculiar conditions of environment, and has also in many places been influenced by historical contacts, but what any system of economy essentially represents at any time is the means that a certain number of people have chosen for living on the resources which they know to be at their disposal. Different systems are therefore evidence of the existence of the factors of production in different proportions, and as Dr. Harrison told the British Association in 1930, we are not yet able to define the nature of "the common faculties of the human mind," nor to distinguish those that have a bearing on the progress of discovery and invention.[1] The assumption that people who manage their production without using machines are savage, and therefore stupid; or that a belief in magic is indicative of superstitious fear while deference to a supernatural religion is a mark of civilization, may be agreeable convictions to some people, but there is no scientific index of correlation between economic and intellectual progress. In some societies money is a measure of individual motives, in others it is not; but because the society using money indulges in a wider range of activities, it is not necessarily more advanced or progressive in any other respect than that of the methods by which it relates the scarcity of its means to the insistence

[1] *British Association for the Advancement of Science, Report of Proceedings,* 1930. Section H, "Evolution in Material Culture."

of its ends. And it is in this respect that we find the criteria of differentiation between backwardness and progressiveness in economic organization. The term civilization, or civilized, has acquired too many extraneous connotations to be of significance in this specific connection; it implies evaluation of the ways in which tools are used as well as of the tools themselves. An advanced economic system is simply one in which the accumulation of capital and the invention of capital-goods make the process of production roundabout instead of direct, and the division of labour increases its efficiency; while a primitive system is one in which the relative deficiency of capital keeps the productive process direct, or from hand-to-mouth, and there is little specialized production for exchange, and hence only limited and clumsy media of exchange.[1]

Any tool or instrument used to assist labour in production is capital, whether it is a digging-stick broken on the way to work and discarded afterwards, a spear carefully fashioned by the owner and inalienably his for ever, or a machine used by a succession of hired labourers who have no share in its ownership; but there are nevertheless extensive differences of degree between the capital goods of primitive and of advanced society. The characteristic they all have in common is that they make the productivity of labour greater than it would have been if employed alone, but under primitive conditions individual effort is directed towards obtaining goods for direct consumption, and there is little specialized production for exchange. Primitive capital, therefore, has very little effect upon the time structure of production. In deciding to make a spear or a bow instead of hunting with his bare hands, primitive

[1] It is frequently said that the absence of specialized production for exchange is the *result* of the lack of a money medium, but there seems to be ample evidence that a convenient unit of account is evolved wherever the need for one arises out of increasing exchange.

man makes a choice between different ways of expending not goods but labour; and since the labourer is his own capitalist and entrepreneur he derives the gain which results from any improvement in production through the redistribution of his effort. Another element of difference is that in a primitive system natural conditions, e.g. wet and dry seasons, the period of crop maturity and so on, are the predominant influence in the time structure of production, whereas in an advanced system this depends to a far greater extent upon the roundaboutness of the technical processes.[1]

Where primitive economy is based on the crop cycle, that is in communities where some form of settled cultivation has replaced the perennial gathering of wild produce, it needs a stock of food for the maintenance of labour between harvests. And this corresponds to capital as John Stuart Mill defined it, "that part of his possessions, whatever it be, which is to constitute his fund for carrying on fresh production."[2] But since the cultivators start again in the same way after each harvest, the capital is not used for the purpose which Adam Smith regarded as the chief function of a stock, namely, to promote the division of labour. In many primitive communities cattle are a treasured form of wealth, but unless they are utilized for draught or dairy purposes—which is seldom the owner's object in acquiring them—it is difficult to classify them as capital. They repre-

[1] This is not an attempt to say that economic progress can change seasons or prevent the weather affecting agriculture. It means that in capitalistic economy cultivation is only one of many stages in the productive process, and while the growing of wheat and hops is seasonal, the making of bread and beer has other technological stages. Schmidt, cit. supra, p. 106, makes the unusual statement, "that form of productive activity which aims at the provision of raw material is called primitive production." The only credible interpretation of this is that under primitive conditions stages of production subsequent to the first are comparatively unimportant.

[2] *Principles of Political Economy*, Bk. 1, Chap. 4.

sent a final end in which savings have been invested, and while as instruments of contract they may facilitate such social processes as marriage, they are no more used for productive ends than are the ceremonial mats of Samoa.[1] Primitive people are no less sensible to the attractions of accumulation than others who have more varied opportunities of acquisition; but in the absence of an exchange economy and a wide choice of consumption goods, more satisfaction is to be derived from the prestige that attaches to ostentation and munificence than from the conservation of a homogeneous stock of possessions past the point of personal repletion.

Because primary production is of predominant importance in primitive economy, however, it must not be assumed that all the productive skill and effort of such communities is devoted to foodstuffs. "Subsistence is in the nature of things prior to conveniency and luxury," but according to our basic definition any occupation is primitive when it is carried on with a marked deficiency of capital, and this is the condition of such indigenous industries as the cloth and leather of Kano, the batik silk of Java, the brasses and calicoes which Europeans discovered in India, and the pottery and lacquer of China. Most of these craftsmen are also cultivators, or at least have some claim upon the land of their family or village, and it is on their relation to the land and not on their technical skill that their social status depends. In India the peasant is of higher caste than the artisan, and in some parts of the Pacific tribes who are forced to obtain their foodstuffs by trading other articles are regarded as inferior.

Under primitive conditions, therefore, the connection of

[1] I. A. Richards, *A Study of Hunger and Work in a Savage Tribe*, says, "food is, in fact, in most primitive societies the only form of capital man has. It is for this reason, I believe, that eatables are so often produced in savage societies in excess of actual needs." (P. 89.)

the whole population with the land is necessarily direct and clear; and in every society there is an established relationship of the people to the land on which they live, a relationship which has evolved to meet the requirements of subsistence under the concomitant conditions of environment, which is embodied in the customary system of land tenure and forms the basis of all productive organization. As a Dutch writer has described it, "Agrarian policy has a dominating significance throughout the colonial world, even if it only takes into account indigenous society itself, because in this society social structure and agrarian conditions form one indivisible whole."[1]

Where the gathering of wild produce is the form of culture and at an elementary stage of cultivation, the land is used as it is owned, communally by the tribe, and there is no delimitation of individual areas. At a more advanced stage of development there is a recognized unit subject to individual or family use, and usually each holder is entitled to an area sufficient to yield an equal amount of produce. Where a patriarchal chieftainship has emerged, or a personal sovereignty has been established, certain areas are set aside for the use of the chief and his family, and the tribe has to provide the labour for cultivating them. Under such a system, although the tribal lands are still communally owned, the use of them is subject to the approval of the chief. Custom, however, recognizes the claim of a cultivator to land which is kept continually in use, and this tenure cannot be arbitrarily interrupted unless the chief is in a position to exercise despotic power. Lawfully he can only resume neglected or abandoned land. In some parts of the East a "joint family" system of tenure has grown up concomitantly with a village type of economy in which there is a distinct recognition of hereditary claims to family land, but usually one member of the group cannot sell his share

[1] A. D. A. de Kat Angelino, *Colonial Policy*, Vol. II, p. 429.

without the agreement of the others. Under tribal economy, however, there is no recognition of individual rights to the ownership of land in perpetuity, and no power of transfer inheres in the cultivator. Since the land is regarded as the basis of social organization and the indispensable source of all subsistence, it is natural that it should not be treated as a freely negotiable instrument, for there is nothing in tribal lore or practice to take its place.[1]

While economic organization everywhere in the tropics is characterized by a lack of capital relative to that of Europe, it is itself divided into two types by variations in the relative supplies of land and labour in different places. In consequence we find what may be described as an African type of economy—although it is found also in other thinly populated areas such as New Guinea and Fiji—in which the population is very sparse in relation to the land on which it lives; and an Oriental type which is characterized by a very dense population on limited land.[2] Both differ from the distribution of agricultural labour in European economy, the African having less and the Oriental having more. But the lack of capital equipment in both is responsible for a low standard of living which leads investors to expect cheap labour, and for an inefficient technique which seems by the measure of advanced economy to waste valuable sources of wealth.

Rice is the chief subsistence crop of the Orient. It supports a larger aggregation of people per square mile than any other tropical food, and demands of them constant and industrious cultivation. Hence a dense population grew up which could only support itself by methodical and continuous labour, and could not rise above a low standard

[1] Orde Browne, *Vanishing Tribes of Kenya*, Chap. II, "Land Tenure," points out also how difficult it is for people who live by a system of shifting cultivation to conceive of the use of land for permanent purposes.

[2] See Appendix A for relative density of population by continents.

of living.[1] Land had become scarce relative to numbers, the marginal productivity of labour was small, and the pressure of consumption demands left little opportunity for the accumulation of capital. The scarcity of free land still enabled the landowner to extract some sort of surplus from the cultivators, but this was spent upon his own consumption or squandered in warfare. Before the introduction of Western capital an increase in rent was difficult to obtain; the increase in population had carried the margin of cultivation to the point of diminishing returns, and hence, when European investment created a demand for labour in new areas, India and China proved to be a great reservoir of mobile wage-earners.

The tree and the digging-stick and the hoe cultures by which the people lived in tropical Africa gave rise to a completely different economic structure. Subsistence crops are in some places yam and cassava, in others millet or maize, and in a few, bananas. Groundnuts are an important article of food over a large area, and up to the time of European penetration forest products were still accessible to most tribes. A dense population could not be supported by these methods, and the African did not feel the same pressure as that of the crowded East to labour continuously for an exiguous return. Land for the most part remained plentiful in relation to population, and labour was the factor of cultivation which was relatively scarce. In the view of the European capitalists who wanted to develop the country, the land was only partially and wastefully exploited; but they did not find the ready supply of native labour which they expected, for in the view of the Africans

[1] E. Huntington, *The Human Habitat*, Chap. VIII, "The Civilization of Rice Lands," gives an impressive list of the qualities and conditions created by this crop, "Wherever rice is raised not only do the standards of living rise and the qualities of thrift and industry increase, but a selection occurs which gradually weeds out those who will not work, and who will not submit to authority." P. 108.

their labour was most advantageously distributed by their extensive methods of cultivation. In South America there was a similar scarcity of population when the Spaniards and Portuguese began to colonize the continent, and the effects of a labour shortage are still conspicuous over extensive tropical areas where Europeans have not settled.[1]

The organization of labour in indigenous economy is primarily determined by the degree of knowledge and skill with which the people can utilize their land. Work can be divided into two classes, individual and communal, the former being food-gathering or cultivation, the building of houses, and the making of household articles, when these are done by the members of the family; and the latter the clearing of forest, the making of roads, the erection of stockades, which are matters in which the whole community has an interest. But even in the produce of individual labour the producer has no exclusive rights of consumption. "The provision of food and lodging, of everything needed to support the existence of the individual members of the community, is treated as a communal matter," and rights of private possession do not extend to the recognized needs of life.[2] Thus the hunter, the food-gatherer, the farmer, must share the surplus which he obtains with his family or village. At the base of this communistic distribution is the idea of reciprocity, every member of a group expects to be able to take something in due course in return for what he gives.[3] But this collectivist basis of recognized needs

[1] E. W. Shanahan, *South America*, p. 64, says "the tropical lowlands of the continent never carried a dense native population such as those of South-East Asia." The indigenous race lived in a most primitive fashion, and "whatever labour force they have been induced or compelled to supply has always been of the most meagre."

[2] Thurnwald, op. cit., p. 186.

[3] F. M. Keesing, *Modern Samoa*, quotes a Samoan of mixed blood on this point of communal claims on property, "Every Samoan is like a

does not preclude personal ownership of objects outside that category which the individual may acquire by skill or chance. The possession and exchange of these is usually, however, carefully regulated. In one psychological division are objects closely associated with particular persons—spears and baskets which they have made, cooking utensils which they use—and these are treated as personal attributes of the owner, as inalienable as any of the vital qualities of life. In quite another division are the other desirable objects, the exchange of which is in origin more ceremonial than commercial, so that the generosity of an individual is expected to be in proportion to his wealth.

The division of labour in primitive society follows family lines, different occupations being allotted to men, women, and children, and to slaves where these are used; but there is little specialized production for exchange outside the group, and in the absence of roundabout capitalistic processes of production there can be no division of labour

banker with credit and debit accounts on his relatives and friends." P. 293.

It is important to realize the exact implications of this communistic system of distribution as compared with that of individualistic capitalism. The two are not as fundamentally antithetical as is sometimes supposed. No society of any solidarity permits its members to fall below the recognized minimum of subsistence. Primitive society differs from advanced, not in making communal provision for these needs, but in lacking wide possibilities of individual gains over and above this level. For one thing, there is in primitive society less difference between public and private utilities, that is, yams are provided in the same way as roads. For another, the principle of the redistribution of wealth between those who do not produce enough for their own needs and those who are held by public opinion to possess too much is applied through a process that is direct, as distribution has to be in an a-capitalistic economy. The possessor of inadequate goods applies to his family instead of to the Government for a supplement, and they reciprocally dispense goods instead of disbursing taxes. And the custom of expecting the munificence of an individual's distribution to be in proportion to his wealth without any regard to the mutuality of exchange values surely embodies the principle of the graduated income tax.

between different stages of production in the sense which the term bears in advanced economy. The individual has in consequence only a narrow range of opportunity cost from which to choose in disposing of his effort, and still another limiting factor in his choice is the customary organization of his tribe. "The impulses governing the nature and direction of work are embedded in the traditions of the group to which the individual belongs. Tradition determines the economic needs and the impulses directed to satisfy them."[1] We have seen that in the African type of economy labour enjoys certain advantages from its scarcity relative to land; and in this as well as the Oriental it is valuable relative to capital, therefore we might expect its disposition in both types to be the dominant factor in the organization of the whole economy.

A few characteristics common to primitive labour in all places and under all forms of political organization can be isolated. WORK IS DONE COLLECTIVELY RATHER THAN INDIVIDUALLY. "Food production in even the most primitive type of society demands organized co-operation," says Dr. Richards. "Even such relatively simple forms of hunting as the setting of snares and game-pits are rarely carried out individually. While the agricultural and pastoral life demand co-operation on a wider scale still."[2] In the next place, the OUTLOOK WITH REGARD TO ACTIVITY AND WELFARE IS COLLECTIVIST RATHER THAN INDIVIDUALIST. The structure of primitive African society, says Major Orde Browne, tends "to stress the importance of the welfare of the tribe rather than the individual; each person learnt to think of himself more as a unit in a group than as a separate entity, and he relied with full confidence on the help of that group in case of adversity."[3] Not only did such organization fail to

[1] Thurnwald, op. cit., p. 209.

[2] I. A. Richards, *A Study of Hunger and Work in a Savage Tribe*, p. 85.

[3] Orde Browne, *The African Labourer*, p. 13.

stimulate that degree of individual initiative which comes of full personal independence and self-reliance, but it also controlled the exercise of individual abilities by its members. "Every Kafir is supposed to be a sort of policeman, and it is his duty to report to his father, or headman, or petty chief any violation of clan interests that he has observed. He is his brother's keeper in fact and not merely in theory."[1] In the East the "joint village" system works under similar conditions,[2] and innovations have been made co-operatively rather than individually.[3] Accompanying all the work in these communities is a BELIEF THAT CERTAIN MAGICAL FORCES WHICH CAN BE INVOKED BY RECOGNIZED RITUAL ARE INDISPENSABLE TO THE SUCCESS OF EVERY ENTERPRISE, and political authority is in some degree everywhere identified with the power of magic over natural forces.[4] This reliance on supernatural assistance, however, does not prevent the labourer from making the most of his own ability; the cultivator does not relax his vigilance because the medicine-man has blessed the crop, on the contrary he is likely to feel it incumbent on him to be more industrious.[5] In this respect magic may be regarded as the primitive form of "put your trust in God, and keep your powder dry." But from another point of view it gives a peculiar character to that element of risk

[1] D. Kidd, *Kafir Socialism*, p. 12.

[2] V. Anstey, *Economic Development of India*, pp. 53–4.

[3] C. F. Strickland, *Co-operation for Africa*, Chap. II, surveys the results in India of Societies for Better Living which could use the collective principles of action to which the villages were accustomed.

[4] Driberg, *At Home with the Savage*, p. 3. Malinowski, *Argonauts of the Western Pacific*, p. 59. From this productive function of magic must be distinguished the part played by the "clever and unscrupulous wizard" who "must be regarded as a thoroughly evil influence," Orde Browne, *Vanishing Tribes of Kenya*, p. 184.

[5] Malinowski, "Primitive Economics of the Trobriand Islanders," *Economic Journal*, March 1921, shows that when the magician has performed a rite on a selected garden plot the owner is "bound to keep pace with the progress of magic, that is, he may not lag behind with his work."

in enterprise which is the source of profits. If in such matters as the production of a good crop or the successful construction of a canoe the primitive labourer sees no difference between practical and magical methods, then the reward for success goes to those authorities who can claim to be responsible for the favourable distribution of magical influences.[1] The final characteristic of primitive labour is that INSTRUCTION IN THE ESTABLISHED ROUTINE OF WORK AND ITS CORRESPONDING RITUAL FORM THE ESSENTIAL EDUCATION OF THE YOUTH OF THE TRIBE, and it is therefore difficult for the rational advantages of a more efficient technique to be introduced from external sources later in life.[2]

The next comparison that we have to make between primitive and advanced economy is in the conditions that determine the use of such quantities of factors as they respectively have. That is, to examine whether any limiting conditions are operative in the relating of means to ends by which a state of primitiveness may be distinguished. This depends on the degree of advantage with which available factors are combined; on the extent to which new knowledge concerning them is utilized; and on the question whether the community makes the maximum use of its resources and knowledge, or whether the rigidity of tradition excludes the adoption of improvements which experience might suggest. "Substance is the static warp and method is the dynamic woof of man's material culture,"[3] and the conditions of primitive economy make it clear that it is in the individual's application of his effort that we must look for dynamics of method. What are the incentives to

[1] In this connection it may be noted that L. H. Buxton, *Primitive Labour,* includes in the chapter on the Division of Labour the "principle of specialization due to leadership," and states that "the principle of the 'wages of supervision' may be said to be very generally accepted among savages." P. 17.

[2] Richards, op. cit., p. 86. Driberg, op. cit., p. 3.

[3] Harrison, *British Association,* cit. supra.

improvement? And correlatively the restrictions upon innovation?

There are two ways of increasing efficiency, a larger amount may be produced with the same effort or the same amount with less effort. The motive for making the change depends upon the reward which is expected to accrue as a consequence of it, and this may take the form of either longer leisure or greater productivity, or a part of both. There is widespread evidence that in primitive society the possession of a large quantity of produce is the source of personal pride and social prestige, and the satisfaction that is to be derived from a munificent display at the end of hunt or harvest must be a decided stimulus to exertion for productive ends.[1] Under nomadic conditions importance attaches to achievement in active enterprise, and "to be first in war or the hunting-field is the crowning honour of life," while in a settled agricultural economy "status depends more largely upon the possession of herds of cattle and well-filled grain bins."[2] But even where no alteration of political status is involved in the possession of property,[3] general recognition of the merit of personal productive ability is sufficient to encourage the individual to make the utmost use of any special skill he possesses. Thus "a good garden worker in the Trobriands derives a direct prestige from the amount of labour he can do, and the size of garden he can till. The title *tokwaybagula*, which means 'good' or 'efficient gardener,' is bestowed with discrimination and borne with pride."[4]

[1] R. Firth, *Primitive Economics of the New Zealand Maori*, "The Feast," p. 329. Malinowski, *Primitive Economics of the Trobriand Islanders*, cit. supra.

[2] Richards, op. cit., p. 109.

[3] I. Schapera, "Economic Changes in South African Native Life," *Africa*, April 1928, points out that among the Bantu cattle were a measure of wealth, but they did not improve the status of the owner in the tribe.

[4] Malinowski, *Argonauts of the Western Pacific*, p. 60.

The reason frequently adduced for the lack of innovation in primitive society is that since the system of distribution is communistic there is no incentive for the more skilful or energetic members of the community to produce more than they can themselves consume. One objection to this argument is the custom mentioned above, that there is a festival and ceremonial character attaching to plentiful display which makes ostentation in itself an end of productive effort.[1] Another, probably even more conclusive, is that hierarchical status emerges from diversity of skill in co-operative enterprise. The conditions of primitive economy necessarily make the connection between productivity and the standard of living very clear; and since this is a matter always important and sometimes urgent, it is not surprising to find that "success in the food quest determines almost universally social prestige in a savage society."[2] Exceptional ability in food-collecting or in hunting practically always leads to political power, and the individual who is found to display a skill in other crafts that cannot be generally copied is regarded as being "the possessor of a beneficent magic,"[3] a distinction that carries both power and privilege. These are merely variations appropriate to the existing circumstances of a situation to be universally observed, that when society realizes some of its wants to be of a higher order than others it offers a higher reward for their fulfilment, and where a relatively greater amount of skill is

[1] Driberg, op. cit., p. 209, "it is obvious that display and ostentation play a relatively important part in social life and . . . make production keep pace with prodigality."

[2] Richards, op. cit., p. 89. Firth, op. cit., p. 164, says of the Maoris, "though skill in all the industrial arts was the object of praise, diligence and expertness in the winning of food did most perhaps to secure the ascendancy of a chief."

[3] Thurnwald, op. cit., p. 134. L. H. D. Buxton, cit. supra, p. 17. And W. Jaspert reported in Angola, "It is often the case with the negroes that the best smith is also the chief," *Through Unknown Africa*, p. 256.

required for some productive activities, these will enjoy a larger measure of importance.[1]

All primitive societies are not communistic. There are more people living under backward conditions of production in caste societies than in communal; and whether a social hierarchy establishes itself from within or is imposed by conquest, it delimits spheres of enterprise for members of different status. It is the fortune—or the fate—of every member of a caste to be born to an unalterable *status quo*, whether he is rich or poor there is nothing more for which to hope; in such a society there is no stimulus to individual enterprise for the sake of self-improvement. Moreover, traditional standards make dignity and leisure rather than change and activity the aim of personal ambition.[2] It has been said of the Malay, "he goes through existence with an easy grace born of long centuries' experience in the art of getting the best of things with the least exertion."[3] This is an ability not to be despised, but its standard of success is largely independent of positive material achievement. It is, however, a very real influence in the orientation of societies both with and without a caste system; and a complementary characteristic which completes the differentiation of these standards of attainment from those of modern Europe is the ideal that "age and rank should be respected and obeyed; precocity or innovation among youth is a social sin."[4]

When a caste system makes manual labour exclusively the occupation of the most degraded section of the community, a check of another kind on enterprise and efficiency becomes operative. It is a familiar observation in every country and among every race that slave labour is the most

[1] Firth, op. cit., p. 158, gives an example of this from dredging for shellfish by the Maori.

[2] Knowles, op. cit., p. 183.

[3] A. Wright and T. Reid, *The Malay Peninsula*, p. 315.

[4] Keesing, op. cit., p. 31.

expensive form of labour because it has least interest in being productive. A similar apathy and absence of incentive is found where a community has become inured to maintaining a precarious livelihood in the face of constant danger from political enemies or natural forces. One reason why the forest tribes of the Gold Coast neglected agriculture was that "the continual inter-tribal warfare in which the people seemed to have been engaged, was opposed to the cultivation of crops which might become an incentive to a covetous attack."[1] And with regard to the frequent remark that the Indian has no initiative, Dr. Knowles has pointed out that "a man is not likely to have developed great initiative under a long series of nature's catastrophes and man's devastations."[2] Indeed, to live as though you are going to die to-night may have admirable moral results, but as a constant condition of existence it discourages material effort.

In explaining the comparative absence of innovations in primitive society Thurnwald says, "It is not sufficient that discoveries should be made by individuals, but such discoveries must be raised by the community to the rank of cultural conditions in order to take effect."[3] But so must they in advanced economy. Only here the process takes place through roundabout methods of marketing, excluded from primitive society by its very structure, for only such inventions can be marketed by individuals as serve socially acceptable purposes. In every type of community there is

[1] G. C. Dudgeon, *Agricultural and Forest Products of British West Africa*, p. 45.

[2] Knowles, op. cit., p. 273. C. F. Strickland, *Co-operation for Africa*, p. 17, gives a similar explanation of the absence of incentive among Indian villagers. And C. A. Cabaton in *Java*, p. 112, says: "Perhaps we should attribute the very real apathy of the Javanese, as of many other Asiatics, to the fact that he has laboured incessantly for centuries, but never for himself."

[3] Op. cit., p. 275.

collective judgment of individual initiative,[1] and that the process is more direct under primitive conditions is in itself no reason for supposing that this type of society is more reluctant than others to adopt innovations that facilitate the attainment of desired ends. The fact that primitive economies do experience long periods of continuity undisturbed by forces of reorganization and change must be regarded primarily as evidence not of their incompetence in utilizing their resources to achieve desired ends, but of the satisfactory adjustment to this purpose of the fixed proportion of factors at their disposal. And if an innovation in methods of production is to be successfully introduced from outside, it must appear a suitable substitute for the old technique in every respect. For instance, a Government official tells how he tried to introduce an efficient double-bladed paddle among a tribe on the Uganda lakes whom he found using a clumsy single-bladed article. But although they admired his innovation they would not use it, for it had not been made with the ritual that would bring success to a fisherman and protect him from the dangers of his calling."[2] And before we dismiss this incident, and many like it, as one of the superstitions of a backward people, we should notice the similarity of the attitude it reveals to that of the British public towards the first steamships, namely, that it was contrary to the will of God to make ships run against wind and tide. No doubt subsequent generations of Uganda fishermen will appreciate the contribution of a better paddle to safety and success just as God-fearing men perceived how useful the addition of steam was to transport, for in the end it is utility that supplies

[1] L. Robbins, *Essay on the Nature and Significance of Economic Science*, p. 93. "We assume a legal framework of economic activity. This framework, as it were, limits by exclusion the area within which the valuations of the economic subjects may influence their action. It prescribes a region in which one is not free to adopt all possible expedients."

[2] Driberg, op. cit., p. 3.

evidence of the will of Divinity. As Graham Wallas said of the discovery of mathematics, "Such thought methods were often held by those who could not understand them to be so unnatural and impious that men were killed for using them. They would, perhaps, have been abandoned by the whole race, but for the fact that the new processes were found to be more effective than the old."[1]

Once the influence of foreign contacts has been felt it is virtually impossible to say whether the effect upon the indigenous economy is due to changes in ends or to new methods of attaining old ends. We shall discuss later the incentive that new ends provide for changing the orientation of labour and production; for the moment we are only dealing with the use made of available factors in meeting established ends. Like the Greeks, the tropical peoples "run their world by hand," and their efficiency or their failure is fundamentally an issue between labour and natural forces. The effectiveness of enterprise in societies of this type is distinctly limited by the rudimentary nature of their capital equipment. And much of the disparaging criticism of races from Fiji to the Congo, whom civilization had forgiven for being heathen but could not tolerate being "indolent," would have been avoided if the implications of the ratio in which they must necessarily combine their factors of production had been recognized. When native organization is considered not relatively to capitalistic, but merely in the light of its internal resources, a different opinion emerges. "Developed systems are based on generations of experience," writes an agricultural expert, "and show a remarkable adaptation to environment. A culture system which appears to be primitive usually proves on examination to be eminently practical."[2] The "mixed garden" system of cultivation which was widespread in the tropics did not conform to modern European standards either in the appearance or the yield

[1] *Our Social Heritage*, p. 36.

[2] C. A. Barber, E.M.B., 2.

of its crops, but it had certain definite advantages for the native which a greater expenditure of effort on more systematic cultivation would, without the addition of other factors beyond his reach, most probably not have secured.[1] "The benefits of mixtures may be summarized by saying that they are those ordinarily attending crop diversification. The possibility of crop failure is diminished, for loss due to insects, for example, will generally be confined to one staple. A mixture tends to distribute work more evenly throughout the season and level out the peaks which occur at certain seasons in one-crop areas. Finally, it takes the best advantage of the soil and the weather in any one season."[2] Another criticism of native agriculture in some regions has been directed at the custom of leaving tree-stumps in cleared land with its consequent interruptions of continuous ploughing, but this was an expedient that served a definite purpose. "The object of retaining the bush stumps and roots in the fields is that, after two or three years of cultivation, the bush may be easily reinstated, and again after ten or fifteen years, when cut down and burnt, it furnishes a supply of wood ash for the fertilization of the field." While the difficulty of using ploughs in such land made them unacceptable innovations, improved hoes and forks were readily accepted.[3]

When European development of tropical territory begins, the balance between labour and natural resources is changed by the addition of capital. All modern improvements in

[1] C. W. Willis, *Agriculture in the Tropics*, p. 29, describes this system in its aspect of a plant society.

[2] Professor R. C. Wood, "Rotations in the Tropics," *Journal Tropical Agriculture*, February 1934.

[3] Dudgeon, op. cit., 17, in reference to Sierra Leone. And F. M. Dyke, *Report on the Oil Palm Industry in British West Africa*, says that Nigerian farmers already crop their palms to the maximum advantage. Hence output would only be increased by more transport facilities and better extractive machinery. Pages 3–4.

the tropics derive from the introduction of new capital in some form, whether an irrigation dam in the Gezira, a canal in India, ploughs in Nigeria, cotton seed in Uganda, or plantation investments in Ceylon and Malaya. The indigenous lack of capital resources is necessarily reflected to a large extent in the scales of valuation that direct the effort of backward people. Nevertheless, these differ not in kind but only in degree from those that direct the use of capitalistic means of production. It is a consciousness of vulnerability by unknown or uncontrollable forces that gives rise to a belief in magic in any society, and superstition performs a positive function in the absence of more tangible measures of security.[1] Every people feels a sense of safety in what is familiar and habitual which makes it reluctant to change old customs for new gains that appear hypothetical. "Defence," said Adam Smith, "is better than opulence," and it is the same sentiment that makes the tropical native reluctant to abandon methods which have long provided him with subsistence in favour of something more progressive but as yet unproved.[2] Moreover, as Professor Whitehead reminds us, "It requires a very unusual mind to undertake the analysis of the obvious."[3] The deficiencies of a society are more readily seen from the outside than the inside; and even if we assume that "primitive man did not

[1] J. G. Fraser, *The Devil's Advocate, or a Plea for Superstition.*

[2] Willis, op. cit., p. 144, says of the Ceylon peasant, "not that he is averse to making money, but he cannot afford risk." On page 47 he gives an example of the misfortune that may be an adventitious result of unscientific experiment. A planter in Ceylon gave some villagers manure for their fields as they could not afford to buy any. The rice plants grew splendidly, about half as tall again as usual; but when harvest-time came it was found that the paddy fly had eaten the content of all the grain. "Whether this was merely a coincidence, or whether it was that the extra vigorous growth of the shoots had made the grains more tender, is uncertain, but the result of that experiment was a disastrous failure, and the villagers there have acquired a prejudice against manuring which may last a century or more."

[3] A. N. Whitehead, *Science and the Modern World*, p. 6.

think at all unless driven by urgent need,"[1] we must add neither does any other man; but it is the urgent pressure of the multiplicity of means and ends in advanced economy that stimulates thought; the consciousness of alternatives makes change, or reform, one of the ends of effort. Bury showed that this "idea of progress" was a phenomenon peculiar to Western Europe and the nineteenth century, it undermined men's faith in the familiar and fixed their hopes on the unfamiliar. It is here that we find the fundamental difference between backwardness and progressiveness, the distinguishing mark of what Lecky called "the European epoch of the human mind." Primitive man sets his ambitions on living up to his ancestors, modern man is confident that he looks down on his from ever-increasing heights—that is one of the things too obvious for analysis.

When we consider the labour situation which confronts foreign capitalism in backward territories, therefore, it is important to remember that these places have already an integrated economy in which all the factors of production are represented. It is misleading to think that because they so patently lack capital, they comprise only the one factor, labour, awaiting more advantageous employment. The population is not comparable to a proletariat which has no alternative to wage labour, for when they are left free backward people have a choice between the conditions of their customary system of production and the terms offered by the foreign employer. This system has in each place been stereotyped according to the relative quantities of factors at its disposal, and demand conforms to traditionally demarcated lines—a condition the opposite of the flexible demand and supply of advanced economy. The particular economic system which arises from the combination of environmental resources is embodied in the tribal institutions, and its extravagances as well as its limitations are sanctioned by

[1] R. Briffault, *The Making of Humanity*, p. 74.

tribal law and custom. Hence when foreign interests attempt to alter the methods of production in the direction of greater efficiency they meet obstruction. What they consider to be only a simple economic adjustment, native opinion regards as a menace to its whole social fabric.[1] It is easy to see that while the native may be willing to make any changes which he perceives to be beneficial within the existing framework of his economy, changes introduced from outside which require the alteration of that framework will appear to be of quite a different order. Economic matters cannot be isolated from the rest of the social system of ideology and sanctions, and when a change in the system of production is of a kind which requires a change in social laws and ceremonies which are regarded as of the utmost importance to the preservation of tribal integrity, it will only be accepted if the tribe realizes that it is impossible or undesirable to continue under the old system. In its economic isolation primitive economy is self-sufficient, self-satisfied, and self-sanctioned. The purpose of foreign penetration is to break down this economic isolation and absorb its resources into the current of international trade, and for this purpose it is necessary that the natives either produce a saleable surplus over their customary needs or convert their self-contained economy to some degree of specialized exchange. They will only do this when their desire for the proceeds of greater productivity is strong enough to cause an increase in labour effort or to accept foreign improvements of their customary methods, and it is by its influence on

[1] Driberg, op. cit., describes the native reaction to his effort to change their paddles as "a belief that I was trying to upset the economic and religious balance of their lives." The habit of regarding foreign economic influences as a danger to the whole structure of national life is not confined to Africans, as we can see by recalling the protests that have been successively evoked in this country by cheap goods from Germany, mass production in America, and cheap labour in Japan.

this desire that the policy of the metropolitan country takes effect.

Political authority can raise native economic activities above their traditional level either by inducement or by coercion, and the policy of imperial Powers towards their subject territories was at first one of undisguised violence and force. Their methods were confiscation and slavery. The former came to a natural end in the exhaustion of supplies, which undermined the position of Spain in the New World and caused the method of exploitation in Java to change from extortion to cultivation; but slavery became more and more entrenched, for it proved to be the most profitable means of production in tropical colonies which the conditions of the time could compass. In the seventeenth century Europe was only beginning to emerge from a state of primitive economy and hand-to-mouth production, and slaves represented the capital of pre-mechanical ages. Slavery had been a recognized institution of previous civilizations and it was no new departure in law or ethics to keep Africans in bondage. But by the nineteenth century opinion had changed and the hardship and injustice implicit in slavery were not considered to be worth any possible utility it might have. The change, however, was not in ethical ideas alone.[1] The progressive development of the economic structure as a whole had confined the lucrativeness of slave-owning to a few limited fields, and even for these it was argued that free labour could be obtained at a profitable wage. After the disorganization of a short period of transition this proved to be true, although in some places East Indian labourers had to be imported to maintain the cultivation of large plantations. But in opening up new territories the metropolitan countries were usually con-

[1] J. Cairnes, "The Slave Power," Chap. II, *The Economic Basis of Slavery*, discusses the high cost of slave labour on plantations and the limits of its application.

fronted with a situation analogous to that which had given rise to plantation slavery in the seventeenth century. There were prosperous tribes in all parts of Africa no more likely to hire themselves to concessionaires as cheap labour than the Guinea negroes had been to migrate to the West Indies at the offer of a small wage for steady work. Compulsory labour might produce less satisfactory results than voluntary, but it was better than none, and so various methods were devised of making the native work although he was free. In many places, especially when the work of development was just beginning, gang labour was the return he had to make for his new political status, and economically it only differed from slavery in not representing an investment by the employer.

Under any conditions the supply curve of labour depends upon the marginal preferences of individuals for different occupations which they are capable of pursuing, and labour is distributed according to the respective opportunities and attractions of the various kinds of work. The individual constructs his scale of preferences out of the alternatives for gratifying his wants which he conceives to be at his disposal. In a free economy his first choice is between working and not working. For the person who of necessity or desire is going to work the next choice is between the different forms of employment available, and he will choose that which offers the highest return for the effort required, that is, the one which in the given conditions appears the most attractive occupation. The value which the individual can set upon his labour depends upon the possibilities of his alternative means of livelihood. And while in primitive society the range of opportunity cost is not extensive, the free native has a position of security from which to appraise the offers of new employment. He will be willing to work for wages when the relative attractions of doing so or of living otherwise reach a point of marginal indifference; and this is not necessarily the point at which the quantitative yields of the two forms of employment are identical, nor is it at any fixed level. Considerations other than remuneration which determine the labour supply curve are a preference for customary occupations in familiar surroundings as opposed to lengthy travel and unusual work such as mining, and the advantages of independent labour at home over the supervised discipline of a foreign plantation. It may seem worth while to refuse wages which are higher than the cash return to independent production when there is no particular need of that extra increment of cash, for the variability of productive effort depends for the most part upon the elasticity of the worker's demand schedule, and it is when the money character of the native's wants increases that the cash value of his output assumes a greater importance. In order to be successful, therefore, offers of wage employment must have two effects. They must change the native's personal scale of valuation in favour of the new employment, and must overcome the strength of the tradition that binds him to customary tribal practices.

The metropolitan powers have not usually relied on a free labour market to attain these results in colonial territories. The labour of the natives is by European standards for the most part not efficient labour, and that it is paid a low wage does not necessarily mean that it is exploited in the economic sense of receiving less than the market value of its productivity; that value is small from natural causes that only training and skill and improved methods of transportation can alter.[1] In the next place, the native

[1] Alleyne Ireland, *The Far Eastern Tropics*, p. 229, gives an example of this situation from American experience in the Philippines. "All favourable comments on Philippine labour come from the towns, the unfavourable ones from the country. . . . In the towns, Philippine labour is chiefly employed by the Government, the Army, and transportation concerns, that is to say, by persons who are not engaged in producing anything for sale; and in the country districts the employment is agri-

labourer is rarely familiar with a contractual relationship to an employer. When he works for someone other than himself, it is from a sense of personal obligation to the beneficiary. Similarly, the communal distribution of the product of his labour is pervaded by a sense of personal relationship which is not operative in a wage contract. And besides being expensive, it would probably take a long time to convert the natives to a wage system by inducement alone, and delay is another costly factor in development. It must also be taken into account that the obstacles encountered by the new system will probably not be the negative ones of lack of economic response alone, there is likely in most instances to be a positive element of political obstruction as well. Wage labour is an ever-present alternative for the individual to the discipline of his tribe and the authority of his chief, and it is, therefore, opposed by powers who—like others elsewhere—have a vested interest in the *status quo*.[1] So it is not strange that instead of waiting for economic inducement to take its course, the foreign capitalist chooses the swift and simple method of invoking political measures to impose obligations that will make the natives work. That is to say, artificial conditions are created which force their scale of preferences to conform to the requirements of foreign employers.

cultural. The Government and the Army can afford to pay an absurdly high rate of wages because the money wherewith to pay the labourers is the product of taxation and not of the labour itself; the transportation concerns, like the Manila–Dagupan Railway, can pay very high wages because they can adjust their rates to meet their expenses. But the agriculturist is in a very different position. He is producing something for sale in the European or American market in competition with other producers of similar commodities; and any considerable rise in the rate of wages makes it impossible for him to conduct his business at a profit, for the price obtained for his product is not regulated by the labour rates of the Philippines, but by the general rate of wages in all countries producing the same class of commodities.

[1] D. Westermann, *The African To-day*, p. 167, discusses this aspect of development.

The native's reluctance to exchange a long period of labour for a comparatively small amount of cash was made possible by the fact that he could easily dispense with the money, but political interference in the form of a money tax will force him to alter his scale of preference to the extent necessary to discharge this obligation. In the same way, if he is arbitrarily deprived of his land, the source of his customary livelihood, he must alter his disposition to work in favour of an employer. And direct pressure upon him either to increase his permanent cultivation, or to deliver taxes in kind, or to perform some specific task will have the same effect without introducing the use of money.

The result of this breach in his traditional production-consumption system is that the native learns new concepts of exchange value and variable needs; and in due course his labour will be regulated by a pecuniary calculus of motivation. With a higher level of wants the margin of his preference scale rises, and only a very close combination between employers could keep his maximum remuneration down to the amount of his tax. Extractive development cannot proceed far without the construction of means of transport and marketing and these need labour for porterage and roadbuilding, and at length for railways and harbours, which is in direct competition with the demands of agriculture. If this growing activity is competitive, the opportunities of employment offered will be increasingly profitable, until the native is earning the whole value of his marginal productivity. But since a primitive labour supply is of a homogeneous order, this value will probably not be of sufficient variation to produce wage inducements corresponding to the natives' scale of preferences for different types of unfamiliar or strenuous occupations. Hence there now recurs in the occupational distribution of labour a similar difficulty to that which confronted the first efforts to obtain a labour supply, that the price to which the natives would voluntarily respond will make the cost of some types of employment unprofitable for the entrepreneur. Moreover, with his acquired knowledge of money and marketability the native may prefer to grow produce for sale on his own land rather than hire himself for wages, and from the point of view of the employer the situation is analogous to that of the first phase of development when labour could not profitably be obtained by inducement—although the economic consciousness of the native is now of a higher order. The problem at this point is not simply that of making the native productive, but of directing him into certain forms of productivity, and in practice this is rarely left to the competition of the open market, but is conditioned at every point by political regulations.

CHAPTER III

CROPS AND METHODS OF CULTIVATION

THE methods of cultivation practised in the tropics can be broadly classified as plantation and peasant systems of production. The plantation is entirely a feature of European penetration and development from the sixteenth century to the present time, and has been based on the grant of extensive lands to foreign owners. The peasant, a communal cultivator, although becoming to an increasing extent an individual landholder, is the immemorial basis of indigenous agriculture; but while his customary cultivation provided only for the consumption needs of his family or village, he has become, under the influence of foreign contacts, a producer for export, an important source of the world's leading commodities.

The difference between the two systems is fundamentally that of large and small units of production, but the *plantation* is not to be identified wholly by area; it is essentially a type of organization, and takes different forms under different conditions. But its organization everywhere is characterized by a uniform system of cultivation under a central management. It is this test of the source of directing authority which can most conveniently be taken to distinguish plantation from peasant production. For the most part it means that the employer uses hired labour on his own land, but it also means that where peasant-farming is done directly under the supervision of the central factory, e.g. in the case of sugar-cane in Fiji, it comes under the plantation system because the cultivator is completely controlled by the agricultural advisers of the factory. Whereas, when a large landowner divides his land between small cultivators on a share-farming basis, e.g. in coconut-growing in the Philippines, and has nothing more to do with them beyond collecting his share of the product, the management is entirely in their hands, and so the system of cultivation approximates more closely to that of peasant than that of plantation organization. And this is the method of classification which we shall use later for distinguishing between the acreage under each system.

Peasant production is carried on by an aggregation of separate smallholders, each of whom cultivates according to his own judgment and reaps the profits of his own skill. Both the area of a holding and the labour employed on it vary considerably, Chinese conditions having the appearance of "an agriculture of pygmies in a land of giants,"[1] while the Philippines Government grants individual homesteads of sixteen hectares,[2] and while all the available soil on a holding is cultivated in Java, there are places in Africa where the peasant holds more than he can cultivate. The area that one family can work varies from three to ten acres, according to the land and crop, and so the proprietor of larger holdings has to hire labour for at least some seasons of the year. There are thus native-owned areas of rubber in Ceylon, cotton in Uganda, and cocoa in the Gold Coast, on which labourers are regularly engaged, but as long as the owner and his family take part in the ordinary work, such areas must be regarded as peasant holdings. When, as has happened with a few very large areas, the owner becomes a landlord who merely directs production, the organization is that of a plantation.

The landlord does not, of course, need to manage his plantation in person. The fashion of absenteeism, which the *haciendados* set in Spanish America, has found popularity

[1] R. H. Tawney, *Land and Labour in China*, p. 6. "Many farms are less than one and a half acres, few are more than five."

[2] *Commercial Survey of Philippine Islands*, U.S. Dept. of Commerce, 1927, T.P. 52, p. 93.

to-day in Uganda, and the appearance of the company carrying on cultivation under a paid manager has merely changed its form. But as long as cultivation is directed by a landholder, individual or corporate, who controls the labour of the cultivators, and bears the financial risks of the undertaking, it represents the plantation system. It is peasant cultivation which is characterized by the personal labour of the proprietor. There are necessarily, however, borderline cases, when a peasant-holding grows large or prosperous, for example, and an owner who previously helped in the actual cultivation begins to do little more than supervise his labourers. And again, in the case of tenant farming, when it may be difficult to tell how far the cultivator is left to his own initiative, and how much he is guided by the advice of the landowner. As statistics are compiled at present, it is impossible to be sure that a uniform distinction is made between different units of production, and the official classification of peasant and plantation cultivation is practically always made on the basis of native and foreign ownership and not of organization. It is extremely difficult, therefore, to reach a definitive classification for the purpose of comparing the geographical distribution of the two systems and their relative productivity. In highland Colombia, for instance, coffee is grown by European settlers on small as well as large *fincas*, and the fact that much of the sugar-cane land in Brazil is held by large owners does not mean that it is under the centralized management which prevails in Cuba. All we can do in such cases, therefore, is to consider the total figures in the light of the general concurrent conditions. Information as to the actual size of native holdings in various territories is scattered and incomplete, and not even continuous records of the total areas cultivated are available for all territories. In the main, statistics are published only of the area alienated to foreigners, or reciprocally that reserved for natives, in the respective countries; and figures of the acreage that is actually cultivated are obtainable only for certain crops.

Crops.—The tropical crops which first entered international trade were those that indigenous peoples grew for their own use, and while some of the chief revenue crops at the present time, sugar and cotton, for example, are an extension of this source, important additions have been made in two ways. European demand has caused the establishment of new commodities such as rubber and sisal which were not previously used by the natives; and the expansion of market requirements has led to old products being acclimatized in new areas. Hence we now have a greater variety of tropical crops entering international trade; many of them have been distributed far beyond their original habitat, and the native proprietor has a much wider choice than in the time of isolation in dividing his effort between food and money crops.

The first important division between the different types of crops now grown in the tropics, therefore, is from the point of view of CONSUMPTION, and classifies them into *subsistence* when they are meant for the personal use of the grower, and *revenue* when they are intended for sale. One of the chief characteristics of primitive agriculture is the large number of different crops which each cultivator grows in small quantities,[1] and even after natives begin to cultivate a market product they continue for the most part to grow also their customary variety of foodstuffs. Thus, in spite of the spectacular increase in exports in recent years, the greater part of agricultural production in the tropics is still intended for direct consumption by the family or village.[2]

[1] R. C. Wood, "Rotations in the Tropics," *Journal Tropical Agriculture*, February 1934.

[2] In Java in 1925, for instance, native food crops amounted to fifteen and a half acres, and native economic crops to half a million acres. Cmd. 3235, 1928. In India jute planted on 3,268,000 acres provides a higher percentage of total exports than grains and pulses on

This comprises grains and pulses of several varieties, predominantly rice in the Orient and millet and maize in Africa, yams, sweet potatoes, cassava, and other tubers, groundnuts, bananas, legumes of various sorts, different oils and condiments such as sesamum, palm and palm kernel, coconut and castor oil, chillies and other kinds of pepper, and sugar; and in subsistence commodities we must also include such things as cotton and coconut fibre when they are used for household handicrafts.

Revenue crops are primarily intended for export. They comprise rubber, sisal, cotton, and various drugs, for which there is no local demand, tea, coffee, cacao, sugar, and palm oil and kernels, which have been extended until the local consumption is a negligible part of the total production, and coconuts, rice, and groundnuts, which have in some areas grown into exports while remaining important articles of local consumption. Jute is still an export commodity, although mills for manufacturing a large proportion of the crop have been established in Bengal, and bananas are shipped from other areas than those where they are a staple food. Besides the foreign market, however, the growth of capitalistic development and European settlement have created in most tropical territories a local market for fruit and foodstuffs, and enabled the natives to sell surplus produce from their tribal or village lands. In Nyasaland, for instance, there has been progress in maize grown on reserves for the open market, and this secured the Government contract in 1928.[1] Moreover, in the neighbourhood of the new towns in

200,000,000 acres. There are some crops, such as coconuts and groundnuts, of which it is not possible to know how much is produced, but only how much enters into international trade.

[1] H. C. Darby, "Pioneer Problems in Rhodesia and Nyasaland," in *Pioneer Settlement*, Co-operative Studies, 1932. Critics of European settlement in backward areas usually ignore this important change in demand, and argue in consequence that if a small amount of native produce which was previously exported across tribal borders has ceased, it has

Nyasaland and the Rhodesias some natives are settling as market gardeners. Before European penetration there were, of course, local markets for the exchange or sale of surplus products over widespread areas in the tropics, and where money has been introduced and production increased, these native markets have grown both in variety and volume.

The next important classification of crops that we have to make is from the point of view of *cultivation*, and in this respect they can be divided into (*a*) PERMANENT, that is plants which after coming to maturity continue to yield crops for a long or indefinite period, the chief examples of which at present are RUBBER, TEA, COCONUTS, COFFEE, CACAO, and OIL PALMS, the natural life of which, if unattacked by disease, ranges up to a hundred years for coconut and oil palms, and possibly also for rubber, although variations are found according to differences of soil and cultivation systems.

(*b*) PERENNIAL, which includes annual crops from the ratoons of a seed plant for from two to ten years, a notable example of which is SUGAR-CANE; and successive shoots without replanting after the first crop is harvested, as happens with BANANAS, SWAMP RICE, and PINEAPPLES.

(*c*) ROTATION crops comprise the largest variety and amount of those grown by small proprietors, and include what are now called annual cash crops as well as the foodstuffs for the cultivator's own use, e.g. grains, pulses, tubers, legumes, cotton, and tobacco. The rotation system developed

been suppressed by the European settlers in the interests of their own production. This argument cannot be seriously adduced until the changes in local production consequent on the appearance of the new market have been analysed. In 1905, for instance, exports of kola nuts from North Nigeria showed a decline explained by the fact "that the people who used to rely on the collection of sylvan produce for a livelihood have found a more lucrative employment in growing foodstuffs for the troops and Government staff, or in working upon Government roads and railways." Dudgeon, op. cit., p. 132.

in order to secure the advantages of crop diversification by sequence instead of mixture, and the factors in choosing the crops have recently been stated by one technical writer as follows: "The first consideration is, of course, the provision of food for the owner and for his cattle, either as cereals, root crops, legumes, or any combination of these. Next come the money crops which enable him to pay his taxes, and purchase salt, lamp oil, and other simple necessaries. The last consideration, the sequence in which the crops shall be taken, can only be settled after many years of experience. Even then, outside considerations may cause a complete modification; for instance, if a new road is constructed in the neighbourhood, it may become profitable to grow an area of soft cane to be sold for chewing, either to the passers-by or for transport on the road to some populous centre."[1] In this last connection it might be remarked that most of the cotton in Uganda is grown by the roadside, and similarly it was along the new roads built in British Malaya that the natives began to grow money crops.

(*d*) CATCH crops are a type of limited but peculiar significance which have arisen as the complement of plantation development in some places.[2] When a large landowner divides his land between cultivators for the planting of a permanent crop, such as coconuts in the Philippines and rubber in Malaya, the cultivator grows between the trees until they reach maturity ground crops, either of foodstuffs or of some easily marketable commodity, e.g. pineapples and tapioca in Malaya or abaca in the Philippines. A smallholder may also grow subsistence crops between young cocoa or coffee. But without careful cultivation the practice may retard or injure the main crop.

The preceding considerations deal with the character-

[1] Wood, "Rotations in the Tropics," loc. cit. supra.

[2] This type of crop is carefully discussed in "All About Coconuts," by R. Belfort and A. Hoyer, Chap. VII, *The Science of Catch Crops.*

istics of different crops as they affect the *income* of the cultivators; there is also the important correlative aspect of the *capital* which various crops require. This depends upon three factors: the yield relative to the area occupied, the length of the period of waiting for returns after cultivation, and the cost and complexity of the equipment necessary for preparing the produce for market. If a single crop must be planted over an extensive area in order to obtain a marketable bulk, it is clearly more suited for a plantation than for peasants. Similarly, if returns from the investment are long-deferred the crop requires finance to an extent that is beyond the capacity of most natives, unless they mix foodstuffs with the growing trees, as many peasants did in the case of rubber in Malaya. But the augmented need of labour may then cause neglect of the main crop. Few products are saleable in the raw state, and while some, e.g. cocoa and copra, can be as efficiently prepared for marketing in small quantities as in large—given equal care and skill—and are, therefore, as suitable for peasants as for plantations, the greater part of the revenue crops at the present time require treatment in a well-equipped factory before they are exported or consumed. It is true that before the plantation entered the field the same crops were grown and prepared by small cultivators and in small quantities, but first the sugar plantations in the West Indies absorbed the early yeoman holdings; then large-scale cultivation of tea in India and Ceylon practically eliminated the peasant product of China from the international market; and now the oil-palm plantations of the East are threatening the native industry of West Africa. Native rubber, crudely prepared, still finds a market, but at a lower price than the estate grade of product. Like cacao and cotton, rubber can be collected over a wide area by the agent of the merchant who will ultimately market it; but sugar-cane must be crushed, as tea must be fermented and the oil of palm fruit extracted, immediately after harvesting. Hence it was the scientific factory method that by proving more efficient than the methods of the small producer gained control of the industry on the spot. An important consequence of this development, however, is that the large investment which the factory represents depends for its profits upon an adequate supply of raw material from the surrounding region, and must either have a reliable supply of labour to cultivate its own land or must obtain regular deliveries from small producers. Tea gardens and rubber estates, for the most part, use hired labour, and so did sugar plantations until recently, but where the central factory system has become highly developed on the latter—in Fiji, Cuba, Mauritius, and Trinidad—the plantation finds it preferable to sub-let a large part of its area to be cultivated by peasants with advice and supervision, and the factory then obtains a large part of its canes for grinding by contract from these growers, and sometimes from others in the neighbourhood who farm their own land. This movement is really one aspect of the question of the cheapness of independent native production as compared with labour in European employ, which we discuss elsewhere. But since many people who think in terms of native welfare have regarded the appearance of foreign investments in backward territory as something of sinister significance, it may be appropriate to point out here that unless the Government interferes through a scheme of monopoly or licences, a factory for making copra into coconut oil in Manila does not differ from one in Hamburg, nor does one that crushes palm fruit in the Congo differ from one that crushes groundnuts in Marseilles. Because a native has to sell his produce to a local capitalist it does not mean that he is more oppressed or exploited than if he were able to sell it to a merchant abroad; if there is competition between buyers for his output, he will get its full market value, just as we saw previously that a labourer would get his full productivity wage from competition between employers; and if a factory has a surplus capacity it will endeavour to obtain further supplies by offering a price that reduces its profit margin to the working minimum. It is when a Government grants a monopoly to one factory, or limits by licence the number of traders who would buy native produce, that it introduces the risk of the grower having to take an unfavourable price with a large margin of profit for the manufacturer or merchant.[1] There is thus no reason for concluding that because a crop needs heavy capital equipment to prepare it for market it is therefore unsuitable for cultivation by peasants. A distinct connection between plantation cultivation and costly equipment has grown up because it is plantations which have evolved the use of the equipment, but if sufficient inducement were to emerge, this would be supplied for peasants also.[2]

The question of the influence of capitalization requirements in determining tenure is, however, to be distinguished from that of the influence of cultivation requirements. When peasants can produce a crop more cheaply it is not necessary for a plantation to grow it at a higher cost because a factory is needed for processing it; it is sufficient for foreign capital to provide the factory. But crops differ widely in the type and technique of farming they require, and in these requirements we may find an indication of whether the small proprietor or the large employer will be the more successful in producing them. Assuming that the crops are intended

[1] Martin Leake, *Land Tenure and Agricultural Development in the Tropics*, p. 36, mentions that in parts of Africa where there were no competing buyers "during the post-war boom traders were in a position to buy maize in the remoter villages on the same terms as had been current in the past, in spite of the great advance in price shown in the maize markets of the country."

[2] To remedy defects of native drying of cocoa in Ashanti, one of the European buying firms erected a drying machine. Dudgeon, p. 53. And the erection of spinneries in North Nigeria by B.C.G. Ass. stimulated cotton cultivation among the peasants. Idem, 140.

for the export market, the varying character of their cultivation demands may be classified as follows:

(*a*) The degree of scientific treatment required in planting, pruning, spraying, and so on in order either to obtain a product of consistent high quality or to prevent the spread of disease and pests.

(*b*) The extent to which the necessity of using hand labour in cultivating or picking puts a premium on individual care and skill.

(*c*) The need of securing both regular supplies and a uniform quality of product over a large area.

(*d*) The effect of seasonal changes on the supply of labour required.

It has usually been thought that a high degree of scientific cultivation was within the capacity of plantations only, an opinion that was no doubt the logical consequence of the fact that plantations were seen to be more enterprising than natives in making experiments and innovations, and that they had the necessary resources for introducing new methods. Further than this, however, it has been argued that the native, being naturally indolent and impervious to scientific instruction, would allow disease to develop among his own crop until it spread and ruined the whole region, and it is on these grounds that the European planters in Kenya have objected to the natives growing coffee. It should also be mentioned in this connection, however, that coffee was a plantation industry in Ceylon when it was exterminated by leaf fungus in the 1880's, and that more recently witchbroom disease has devastated not the native cacao trees in West Africa, but the estates in Ecuador. Knowledge does not follow naturally from a particular type of tenure, it has to be acquired for a definite purpose, and it is true that the ignorance of scientific methods on the part of natives was a real obstacle to new development until the Government realized the possible value of their production and began to make available to them information regarding cultivation improvements, seed selection, and pest control, which was the result of research and experiment.[1] Next door to Kenya natives are growing coffee in Tanganyika and Uganda with success; bunchy top disease among abaca trees is kept under control by the supervision of the Philippines Government; and although United States cotton has been the prey of the boll weevil in many regions, native cultivation of the crop in Nyasaland has replaced plantation.

In spite of scientific progress, however, the skill of the cultivator and his personal interest in his work are still of great importance, especially for those crops which are least adapted to handling by large-scale machinery. Tea is a notable instance of an export crop which needs much industrious labour both in cultivation and plucking, and cotton, coffee, and bananas are products whose quality can be greatly injured by careless picking and handling, a contingency from which coconuts are practically free. As a consequence of the conditions of slavery and forced labour, the opinion was formed in some places that natives were not satisfactory labourers for crops that required individual skill or judgment; cotton picking, for instance, is not as easy to regulate and supervise as cane cutting, and therefore peasants are likely to get better results from cotton-growing than plantations. It is probably true of smallholders in any country that they are willing to expend more effort on their own account than they would expend for the same return on behalf of an employer, and so it may pay peasants but

[1] C. A. Barber, E.M.B., 2, cit. supra, points out that in the British colonies "when a Government has attempted to render assistance, we find that in the great majority of cases it is the European agriculture which has been favoured while that of the natives has been left to look after itself." This example applies chiefly to pre-war practice in the plantation colonies in the East, and later to Kenya. Where peasant development has become a policy, native agriculture is assisted.

not plantations to grow rice, groundnuts, or cotton.[1] But it is not independence alone that can stimulate care and skill in labour, and it is the function of an employment policy to maintain the individual's interest in his work. To some extent this has been done by the introduction of task labour, the basis on which the United Fruit Company organizes the cutting and transport of bananas on its Central American plantations, and on which most rubber plantations organize the tapping of trees.

One of the primary conditions of retaining a large foreign market is that the producers supply regular quantities of standard quality reliably graded, and it was doubted at first whether a supply conforming to these requirements could be obtained from a large number of separate small production units. But by supervising the selection of seed used for planting, the Government has been able to secure a uniform quality of cotton in Uganda, Nyasaland, and Nigeria; the French Government has used the same method to improve groundnuts in West Africa, and in practically every colonial territory selected seed or seedlings of the major crops are distributed now by Government agricultural stations. Besides, the grading of some products for market is carefully regulated, as in the case of abaca; while in some places the natives are forming co-operative associations for collecting and marketing different products, and as they learn to appreciate the premium that attaches to a particular quality, Government interference with their methods should become less necessary.

Before we judge the merits of native production from the point of view of quality, however, it must be taken into consideration that there is usually a market for other quali-

[1] This is why tobacco is suitable only for smallholders in India, Ceylon, and Malaya, *B. E. Survey*, Vol. V, *Tobacco*. Cf. Duff, *Cotton Growing in Nigeria*, p. 63, for discussion of difference in quality between the work a man does on his own account and that he does for a wage.

ties of product than the highest; and in supplying the demand for cheaper grades the peasant need not prove a less efficient producer than the plantation.[1] It is entirely a question of profitability at a certain price, and it may not pay the plantation to sell the grade the native does. At the same time, it is not to be assumed that native production is necessarily of inferior quality. The highest grade coconut oil, for example, comes from the native plantations of Coorg.

The final factor that may favour one form or another of tenure is the character of the labour supply required by different crops. It is easier to organize plantation production when the work can be fairly evenly distributed throughout the year, as in the case of rubber and sisal. When an annual or semi-annual harvest requires the temporary increase of the labour force to an appreciable extent, as with cotton or coffee for example, difficulties in recruitment are likely to occur; they have, indeed, constantly overshadowed, and in some places delimited, large-scale cultivation of such crops as cacao and coffee in all the South American countries; and one of the problems that will recur with an improvement of production in the East African colonies is how a peasantry, themselves growing seasonal crops, can at the same time provide a reserve labour force for plantations in the peak

[1] The finest quality of cotton grown is the Sea Island variety, which is cultivated by plantations and to a lesser extent by peasants in the West Indies. Some years ago it sold for nearly three times as much as standard American varieties, but the growth of cheap artificial silk has almost extinguished the market for it, while the cheaper varieties of cotton continue in demand.

A somewhat different aspect of the marketability of inferior quality is shown by the refusal of traders in the Gilbert and Ellice Islands to offer a higher price for large copra because the small pieces, although defective in quality, were more easily packed for shipment. *Colonial Report*, 1929–30. And Dudgeon, op. cit., p. 56, states that the merchants regarded Gold Coast cacao as "adapted for the manufacture of a cheap form of sweetmeat, and that if the quality were improved and the price raised in consequence, damage would be done to a new and rapidly growing trade."

season. For the smallholder the problem of these seasonal changes in labour requirements is settled by the choice of a rotation which distributes the work of cultivation and harvesting as evenly as the factors of climate and weather allow. And for the special occasions that still arise, such as the drying of cacao and the picking of cotton, he merely uses more family labour than usual. This is one example of the way in which a plantation might be said to have higher labour costs than a native.

Besides differing in their seasonal requirements as to quantity of labour, crops also differ in the type of labour they require. The hoeing and weeding of nearly all crops can be done by women, but the cutting of sugar-cane and sisal is regarded as being distinctly men's work, and the tapping of rubber trees has so far been done only by men. The harvesting of several other crops, however, although it requires care and industry, is what is sometimes called "light work," and so suitable for women and children; and it is these crops, cotton, coffee, most varieties of pepper and spice, and to a lesser extent cacao, which are best adapted to cultivation on a family basis. Tea is another crop which shares all these qualifications, but for other reasons it has become a plantation industry, and so immigrant labour has been encouraged to settle on the gardens in family groups, and men, women, and children are employed on the tasks that suit them best. For the heavier crops plantations find it sufficient to have gangs of men on short contract periods. But even when a crop is not adapted to family labour, the peasant may still grow it on parts of his land while the other part is used for subsistence crops to which his family can attend.

When we examine the actual distribution of the leading crops between large- and small-scale tenure in the various producing areas we find them divided into four categories. COFFEE, SISAL, SUGAR-CANE, and TEA are the only export products of which the plantation system retains a virtual monopoly. In the category of exclusively peasant crops are GROUNDNUTS, RICE, SESAMUM, and JUTE, which are indigenous products that have expanded to provide an export surplus; while with Government encouragement COTTON has become almost entirely a native crop in regions within the tropics. Thirdly, of the other ancient indigenous crops which have increased to meet foreign demand, COCONUTS are cultivated by plantations as well as peasants in the same areas; but the distribution of OIL PALMS is regionally distinct, except in the Belgian Congo. TOBACCO is grown by both natives and plantations in the Netherlands Indies and Nyasaland, but for the rest of its widespread cultivation the forms of tenure are geographically separate, and while BANANAS come very close to being an exclusively plantation product, the pre-existing forms of tenure and favourable financial organization have enabled smallholders also to cultivate them in Jamaica. Finally, of the comparatively new cultures for export, CACAO is grown by plantations in South and Central America and by natives in West Africa, while both types of cultivation are found in the West Indies. And in the spectacular development of the newly established crop, RUBBER, natives have taken as large a share as estates in the same regions.

The technical factors that have influenced this distribution are the relative cheapness of production of large and small units, and the comparative advantages that one form of occupation or the other offers to a limited labour supply. We have already discussed the relation of capital requirements to the form and organization of primary sources of production, and it is clear that it is in the crops which need extensive factory equipment for processing at the place of origin that the plantation system maintains its dominance. Sugar-cane must be ground, as palm fruit must be crushed, and tea withered, immediately it is cut; and similarly, bananas must be shipped under suitable conditions as soon as they are picked. On the other hand, groundnuts and palm kernels can be stored without detriment to their oil content, and rice keeps well in the *padi*. Sisal needs expensive decorticating machinery, and has to be handled in large quantities, while jute is beaten and dried in small amounts by peasants. The peculiar suitability of cotton for native cultivation is in large measure due to the ease with which it fits into a rotation with food crops. Coffee, which resembles cotton closely in its labour, cultivation, and capital requirements, is, however, lacking in this advantage for peasants. Coconuts require little attention after the young trees begin to grow, hence they are a convenient addition to peasant food crops, and the low labour cost of cultivation makes them suitable for plantations also.

But the single factor of capital requirements does not explain the distinct geographical differentiation in the system of cultivating some of the same crops, nor provide the reason why a plantation and factory should operate in some places through contracts with smallholders, and in other places work its own land with hired labour. We must look to other factors, therefore, for an explanation of why sugar factories in Java hire native land on which to grow their crops while in Cuba factories buy the canes of small farmers; why oil palms have been planted by plantations in Malaya and Sumatra while the industry in Nigeria remains in the hands of peasants, and in the Belgian Congo foreign factories make contracts with the natives besides cultivating areas of their own; and why cacao should be eminently suitable for peasants in West Africa, be monopolized by plantations in Ceylon and Ecuador, and be grown under both forms of tenure in Trinidad. In determining the form and size of agricultural undertakings technical factors are rarely fully operative. Political conditions have not permitted perfect competition between peasants and plantations because one system or the other has frequently been the end of Government policy instead of a means to the end of cheapest production. The influence of such policy becomes clear as soon as we look at the conditions of land tenure under which cultivation is carried on in various regions.

Where large grants of land were made to its own settlers by a foreign Government which established control over a tropical region, a system was established which has determined the form of development for centuries. The influence of the Conquistadores is still to be seen very clearly in South America, and the plantation system of the West Indies is based on the Royal Patents of the seventeenth century. Such grants were made for the purpose of extending national power abroad, and of obtaining profitable sources of raw material; and that there was any other method of fulfilling these ends than by establishing a class of European landowners was not realized by the framers of Imperial policy until comparatively recent times. The establishment of the cultivation of revenue crops by large numbers of peasants is as much a political characteristic of twentieth-century policy as the establishment of the plantation system was of seventeenth-century policy. Rival European Powers started by acquiring land in the tropics, they are now trying to consolidate peoples.

It is true that the extension of capital investment and development programmes in tropical areas, notably those in Africa, revealed that there was on the whole a scarcity of labour where Europeans were accustomed to thinking there was an illimitable reservoir; and besides curtailing hopes of cheap labour on the part of individuals, this made it necessary for the Governments concerned to consider how the largest measure of native productivity might be secured. But when it wanted to, political authority has made some remarkable population movements coincide with other policies. The two million acres of tea gardens in Assam, for instance, are peopled with immigrants, and twelve million acres in the Kenya highlands were cleared of their native population and turned over to Europeans in a few years. Peasant cultivation has succeeded because it was Government policy that it should, and the natives have been given all the assistance necessary for success. Racial and hereditary aptitudes, of course, still mean a great deal. It seems to be as difficult to stop a Chinese coolie in the Straits Settlements from rising in the economic scale as it is to make a Singalese peasant save some capital; and even if the Masai had been encouraged, it is doubtful that they would have become as agricultural as the Baganda. But the Masai, as well as the Kikuyu, who were agricultural, have lost their former fertile lands because the ideas of the seventeenth century revived in Kenya in the twentieth; and the Gold Coast is a territory of active smallholders instead of a country of dormant large ones like Brazil because it became British policy in the twentieth century to develop native landowners as well as native land. And it is entirely a matter of policy that the Chinese may exercise their talents in Malaya, but are not allowed to participate in the extension of plantations in Papua or the Philippines.

In connection with the general subject of organized crop production we should notice also the remarkable geographical distribution of crops that has been brought about in the endeavour to adapt commercial supplies to political frontiers. Except for jute and abaca and a few drugs and spices no commodity of international importance is now obtained exclusively from its indigenous source, and even products for local consumption have been widely acclimatized. Three broad trends can be traced in the course of acclimatization: the first, from the Orient to the New World in the seventeenth and eighteenth centuries, chiefly under the influence of the Portuguese; the next, which started in the late nineteenth century and has continued to recent times, is from the Americas to the new regions of Africa which were being developed; and finally, there has in a few products been a move from American and African habitats to areas of cultivation in the Orient.

I. SUGAR-CANE, which is supposed to have spread from China to India, was taken from there to Brazil by the Portuguese. While it is probable that there was an indigenous variety in the West Indies, it had not been utilized until methods of expressing the juice were introduced from the East.

COFFEE starts its history with a legend of its discovery by priests in Abyssinia, and up to the seventeenth century it was supplied to Europe from Yemen in Arabia, home of the famous Mocha, and from there taken to the West Indies and South America. Attempts to acclimatize the crop in Ceylon were cut short by disease, and with the enormous increase in consumption in the late nineteenth century, Brazil became the largest source of supply, and for many years dominated the world market. This position she has now lost through the increase of production in other places; and in Africa the crop has been encouraged for the markets of the respective metropolitan powers.

TEA was first introduced into Europe from China, and between the seventeenth and nineteenth centuries consumption increased enormously. The discovery of a similar plant in North-East India stimulated efforts to produce the leaf there, and a rapid expansion of cultivation followed in Ceylon and Java as well as in India, which now supply most of the tea of commerce.

CLOVES were once a monopoly of the Moluccas, carefully guarded by the Dutch. But the French succeeded in introducing them into Mauritius, whence the Arabs took them to Pemba and Zanzibar, which are now the chief source of the world's supply. But although GINGER was introduced into the West Indies and Africa from the East, these have supplemented the original source without supplanting it.

RICE is now cultivated far beyond its original Asiatic habitat, and not only where Orientals have settled, but as an addition to the roots and fruit of Africa. Most of the exports, however, still come from Burmah and Siam.

II. CACAO was found growing in tropical America by the Spaniards and Portuguese. It was then introduced into the Portuguese islands off the West African coast and Ceylon, both of which became important areas of cultivation. More recently, however, the crop has been adopted by the natives of the British West African colonies and protectorates, especially the Gold Coast, and these now export as much as all the older sources together.

COTTON of some variety was an indigenous plant of most tropical areas, but it produced a fibre too short for the mechanical spinning of Europe. Hence the longer "American upland" and "American middling" have been introduced in those African territories which now grow cotton for export.

TOBACCO is another crop of American origin with a lucrative European market which has been introduced with success into Africa.

III. CINCHONA was first known as a forest product of Peru, and from there it was introduced into Ceylon and cultivated with success. With careful selection of trees the Dutch East Indies have succeeded in producing a bark with a still higher alkaloid content. Efforts are now being made to establish the tree in the Belgian Congo.

OIL PALM was first recognized as a commodity of importance in the "palm belt" of West Africa, where the extraction of the oil was for a long time a native industry, but the tree is now being cultivated with success by plantations in Malaya and the Dutch East Indies.

One factor in this constant process of acclimatization has

been the desire for political security: from the point of view of the Government, security of a supply of materials which were the necessary complement of its national industries; and from the point of view of the private investor, security for his capital in distant regions. In the first place, the European Powers scrambled for the colonies which produced the commodities they wanted, then when demand changed they had to try to establish the new products in the colonies; hence the "counterpart-to-the-metropole" theory of development so prominent in modern French policy. And while the investor would rather choose for development a territory where he was more likely to be vindicated by a punitive expedition than victimized by a civil war, he has had to adapt his enterprise to a great extent to the available supplies of labour. Thus we find industries swinging back to the East after being discovered in more spacious regions, not only because political conditions were uncertain in those regions, but because workers there were scarce, while the East is still teeming with cheap labour.

While the attitude of Government to land tenure is a primary factor in determining the system of production, the actual extent of cultivation must depend upon the supply of labour in relation to the land.[1] The cost of labour to a

[1] H. M. Leake in "Studies in Tropical Land Tenure," *J.T.A.*, August 1932, et seq., suggests the following tests of the suitability of a crop for a particular kind of tenure:

1. The crop yield, which, however, must be judged in the light of its cost.
2. The quality *intrinsic* to the plant, i.e. by what method of cultivation can the purity of the crop be maintained.
3. The quality *extrinsic* to the plant, i.e. the treatment required by the raw product.
4. By what form of tenure will the capital needed be attracted?
5. What unit or method of cultivation is most likely to give protection from crop disease?

It is noticeable that the relative supplies of labour available for

plantation will increase according to the amount of the native's independent earning power and his measure of preference for being independent, or perhaps for living in his village rather than on a plantation. It is a cost that might easily become prohibitive unless the native's independent earnings are very small, or the plantation grows a much higher priced crop than the native which can pay higher wages. And it is significant that it is in the countries of dense population that both large proprietors and small grow the same crops, while where labour is scarce the same culture seems to be possible only by one method or the other. In the Netherlands Indies, where Java and Madura are the most thickly peopled colonial area, plantations as well as natives grow rubber, tobacco, tea, coffee, and coconuts, and the factories use native land for sugar-cane in rotation with other crops; while in Malaya and Ceylon estates have been able to grow rubber only with the assistance of immigrant labour. Similarly, bananas are grown by small as well as large landowners in Jamaica, but only by plantations in Colombia where population is scantier. With official encouragement of native cotton in Nyasaland the plantations have gradually dropped the crop; and now that the natives are also growing tobacco there appears to be a diminution of that culture on plantations in favour of an increase of tea. Correlatively, we find that while plantations grow sugar-cane and coffee in Uganda they do not compete with the natives in cotton—the large areas of which belong to indigenous landowners. In Ceylon and Malaya, however, where an ample supply of immigrant labour was available, plantations have been able to carry on the cultivation of coconuts alongside of peasants. The great coffee exporting

different purposes is omitted from this examination. It is quite possible for a governmental authority to ignore this factor in deciding on a policy of development, but the execution of the policy will not escape its implications. The other considerations have also been dealt with in the somewhat different arrangement of this chapter.

areas of South and Central America have been developed entirely by alien landowners, and in other places native participation in the crop is comparatively recent. In Java and Tanganyika peasant cultivators appear to have been successful, and while in the former island there is sufficient labour for every type of occupation, it is too early to see what the effect of competition will be in the latter territory.

APPENDIX TO CHAPTER III

ORGANIZATION OF PRODUCTION OF PRINCIPAL TROPICAL CROPS

Over extensive areas of both Africa and South America the banana is an important indigenous food, but no statistics of production exist for these. The export industry has been established in areas where the fruit was not previously of

(*Exports in Quintals*)*

CROP	COUNTRY	PEASANT	PLANTATION
BANANAS	Brazil	—	1,417,480†
	Colombia	—	2,260,781
	Costa Rica	—	1,166,800†
	Cuba	—	766,215
	Guatemala	—	1,160,961
	Honduras (1929)	—	5,371,100†
	Jamaica‡	—	4,919,320†
	Panama	—	797,991

* Figures for 1930 from *I.Y.A.S.* The other large exporting area is the Canary Islands, shipments from which included 2,230,000 quintals to Spain.

† Converted from bunches at the rate of 100 bunches equal 20 quintals.

‡ About one-third of the total from this island represents the production of peasants.

much importance, and has been made possible by the development of cheap refrigerated transport. It is an easily cultivated crop—although much scientific investigation has been expended upon the development of suitable types for export—and the cut bunches must be carefully handled, while it can also be grown in conjunction with food crops and cacao; but the thorough organization and specialized transportation necessary for exporting the fruit have caused it to develop as a plantation industry. The production of the United Fruit Company of America and the Standard Fruit Company in Central America represent probably the most highly capitalized undertakings in tropical agriculture.

About one-third of the crop from Jamaica is shipped by the Banana Producers' Co-operative Association, which consists mostly of small proprietors, and they had sufficiently compact producing areas and enough financial resources to parallel plantation organization and obtain their own ships. At the present time bananas do not keep well for more than seventeen days in transit, so they have to be brought to the European market in fast ships, but this does not mean that the grower must necessarily own his special vessels. The French fruit from Conarky, for example, is shipped in the refrigerated space of ordinary mail liners, and so is Jamaican fruit for Canada. Where cultivators could contract to deliver regular supplies, they should have no difficulty in obtaining shipping facilities at a reasonable rate.

The cacao crop is in many respects suited for cultivation on small scale by a large number of peasants. Food crops can be grown in between the young cacao trees, the pods are easily picked when they ripen, and the whole family can help in opening and drying the beans, while polishing them by "dancing" is a stage of preparation for which children are distinctly useful. Once cacao is prepared it does not deteriorate with keeping, and small quantities can be bought and bulked by merchants. But in order to maintain a high market quality the beans must be carefully fermented, thoroughly dried, and protected from subsequent wetting, and it was because West African native cacao got "mould" from neglect of these precautions that the planta-

CROP	COUNTRY	ACREAGE*	
		Peasant	Plantation
CACAO	Gold Coast (including Togoland)	1,000,000	—
	Nigeria (including Cameroons)	118,332	—
	Fernando Po	—	74,000
	French Equatorial Africa	—	50,000
	French West Africa	—	130,000
	French Cameroons	—	60,000†
	Brazil	—	690,000‡
	Ecuador	—	200,000
	Grenada	20,000§	—
	Trinidad and Tobago	—	220,000‖
	Venezuela	—	180,000
	Ceylon	—	34,000
	Peru	—	30,000

* Figures for British colonies from Statistical Abstract for the British Empire, for other areas from *I.Y.A.S.* All refer to 1930.

† Mostly owned by native chiefs.

‡ Including small proprietors in the Bahia district.

§ Including a few plantations, none of them large.

‖ Including a small number of peasant producers.

tion product has been able to command a premium in the market.

The coconut palm is the indigenous source not only of an important foodstuff but also of many article sof clothing and household use in the whole Pacific basin and along the shores of the Indian Ocean. It also grows wild on about four thousand miles of South American littoral and a long section of the East African coast. It is consumed locally in greater quantities than are exported, and it has remained to a great extent a native crop. Scientific attention has done much to improve the yield of the trees by proper spacing and weeding, and it is impossible to do more than estimate the total quantity of coconut products available in the form of nuts, copra, oil, and coir. Exports, of which figures are available, are probably not more than half this total, to which plantations contribute only about 10 per cent, although they account for a much higher proportion of export figures.[1] The trees take five to seven years to come into bearing, but while they

CROP	COUNTRY	ACREAGE	
		Peasant	Plantation
COCONUTS	British Malaya	400,000	200,000
	Ceylon	913,400	162,800
	India	1,377,000*	
	Netherlands E.I.	1,207,000	127,583
	Philippines	1,407,000†	—
	British Solomon Islands	—	62,400
	Fiji	—	130,772‡
	Gilbert and Ellice Islands	20,000	—
	Papua	30,000	49,000
	Mandated New Guinea	—	198,000
	Tongan Islands	54,400	—
	Western Samoa	41,000	13,000

* Excludes some States for which returns are not available, but none of them are important producing areas.
† Includes a number of "share-farmers" of large individual holdings.
‡ Includes native areas of communal plantations.

are growing food crops can be planted or animals grazed among them. Climbing the trees to pick the green nuts is an occupation that calls for special skill, but for the most part the fruit is left to fall when it is ripe. The trees require little cultivation, which recommends them to peasants, while the consequent low labour cost makes them attractive to plantations, and the copra can be cut and sold as easily by one type of producing unit as by the other. This is one of

[1] K. Snodgrass, *Copra and Coconut Oil*, 1927.

the few crops that both large proprietors and small have cultivated in the same places for a long time. It is to be observed, however, that this is not a measure of their

CROP	COUNTRY	ACREAGE	
		Peasant	Plantation
COFFEE*	Brazil	—	8,000,000
	Colombia	450,000	—
	Costa Rica	130,000†	—
	Cuba	127,000†	—
	Guatemala	—	250,000
	Jamaica	—	5,000
	Mexico	220,000†	—
	Nicaragua	100,000†	—
	Salvador	—	210,000
	Venezuela	—	250,000
	India	—	160,000
	Netherlands East Indies	‡	320,000
	Belgian Congo	—	80,000
	Kenya	—	98,874
	Madagascar	—	130,000
	Tanganyika	§	—
	Uganda	—	39,214‖

* Figures from *I.Y.A.S.* for 1930.

† These are mostly *colono* holdings, but the figures include a few large plantations in each country.

‡ Figures of native acreage are not obtainable, but native exports were 542,361 quintals as compared with 403,129 quintals from the European acreage.

§ Figures of acreage not available. Native exports were 7,000 tons and are on the increase.

‖ A further area, mostly native, is inter-planted.

competitive advantages in export, because in these areas the native product is used predominantly for local consumption, e.g. Malaya and Ceylon, while in most of the native exporting areas, e.g. Gilbert and Ellice and Tongan Islands, foreign plantations are relatively unimportant.

Coffee, an ancient crop of the Near East, has been developed by plantations in regions far from its original habitat. Although efforts have recently been made with success to grow it in new areas, the bulk of exports still come from a few large but well-demarcated regions where climatic conditions are particularly favourable to the crop. To obtain a good quality product the young plants must be carefully cultivated, and the berries picked as they ripen. Care must also be given to the pulping and drying of the beans, but with selected plants and equally favourable weather conditions for picking and drying, the crop can be grown as well in small units as large. Moreover, the character of the harvest makes it particularly suited for family labour. That it is grown to such a large extent by plantations must be attributed to the conditions under which it was introduced into new areas, and the system of landholding that prevailed there, and not to the technical requirements of cultivation.

Cotton has grown from immemorial times in many regions and of many qualities. The indigenous product of India, Africa, and South America was a short fibre which proved unsuitable for the mechanical methods of spinning that developed in Europe, and the long Sea Island cotton which overcame these deficiencies was grown on the early estates in the West Indies. The main source of European supplies for a long time, however, was the "Cotton Belt" in the south of the United States, and only recently has this region lost its dominance in the international market to the new areas of Africa. Egypt, and the Sudan, growing a similar medium fibre, were the first competitors of the United States, and more recently the imperial Powers have all endeavoured to encourage cotton-growing in their respective African territories. This is the reason for the native acreage in Uganda, Nyasaland, and Belgian Congo. Indigenous native cotton was in most places a permanent plant, and frequently mixed with other crops, and in Africa, India, and South America this short fibre is still grown for domestic use. But the fine quality export cotton is an annual crop, and the prime requirement in growing it on a large scale is to keep up the quality of the seed. Once this is done the plant can easily be cultivated and the crop picked by small proprietors, and the product can be ginned and baled at central depots.

CROP	COUNTRY	ACREAGE	
		Peasant	Plantation
COTTON*	India (1929–30)	27,000,000	—
	Brazil	1,400,000	—
	Mexico	300,000	—
	Peru	—	330,000
	Belgian Congo	350,000	—
	Nigeria	†	—
	Nyasaland	30,000	200
	Southern Rhodesia	—	3,000‡

* Figures from *I.Y.A.S.* for area under the crop in 1930. At that time the United States was growing 44 million acres, and in spite of a decrease since is still the largest producer. The estimated area in China was 5 million acres.

† Figures of native area not available. Crop amounted to 43,925 bales of 400 lb. each. *E.C.G.C.* Review.

‡ This is a decrease from 66,000 acres in 1925.

Moreover, since the rapidity of picking, and care in keeping the lint free of dirt and adulterant, depends largely upon the interest which the labourer takes in his work, it is a crop in which the small independent producer is likely to have an advantage over plantations.

Abaca produces the Manila hemp of commerce which has been a monopoly that provided one of the chief exports from the Philippine Islands. Like other crops there, it is grown both by peasants and by share-farmers on large estates. Government experts conduct experiments as to the best methods of cultivation, and supervise the grading of the fibre for export. Although machinery has been introduced for softening and separating the fibre, the crop still requires a great deal of heavy labour.

CROP	COUNTRY	ACREAGE	
		Peasant	Plantation
Fibres—			
ABACA ..	Philippines	1,212,000	—

Jute is another example of a commodity which has expanded enormously and still remained a virtual monopoly of the region of its origin. Moreover, in spite of the commercial importance it has attained, the crop is still cultivated by smallholders in Bengal by methods that involve a great deal of hand-labour, and frequently unhealthy working conditions. An attempt has recently been made to grow the fibre on modern scientific lines in the Belgian Congo, and the experiments are said to show promising results.

CROP	COUNTRY	ACREAGE	
		Peasant	Plantation
JUTE ..	India	2,000,000 (reduced from 3,268,000 in 1929)	—

Sisal crop is a comparatively new entrant into the international commodity market, where it has become a serious competitor of abaca in the manufacture of cordage. Except in the Yucatan peninsula of Mexico where it is indigenous, and from which area it was introduced into East Africa by the Germans, it has proved to be a plantation and not a peasant crop. An extensive area is required to produce a marketable amount, and expensive decorticating machinery to remove the fibre from the stem. The plant requires little cultivation, but it has to be cut by hand, and the accompanying scratches and bruises make the labour unpopular with the natives. Moreover, it offers no opportunity for family labour, and as the leaves are cut throughout the year no difficulty arises over labour for a peak season.

CROP	COUNTRY	ACREAGE	
		Peasant	Plantation
SISAL*	Mexico	88,000 tons†	—
	Netherlands E.I.	—	66,000 tons‡
	Tanganyika	—	390,000 acres (49,926 tons)
	Kenya	—	138,120 acres (15,939 tons)
	Mozambique	—	11,400 tons‡
	Nyasaland	—	9,296 acres (1,300 tons)

* S. G. Barker, *Sisal*, E.M.B., 64, 1933. Tonnage figures are for exports. Both these and acreage refer to 1930.

† Figures of acreage are not available. Indians grow the crop on their own land, and most of the output is now processed by factories under other ownership.

‡ No figures of acreage.

The oil palm is an indigenous tree of West Africa where it has long supplied the natives with an important foodstuff. It has grown without cultivation in a clearly demarcated forest area, and the oil and kernels of commerce were first supplied by natives who picked the fruit and expressed the oil by crude hand methods. But as the oil grew in commercial importance the Belgians in the Congo and the Germans in the Cameroons granted foreign concessions in the palm belt in order to increase production. Large tracts have been cleared of undergrowth and new areas planted, with the result that the yield of fruit is better, the bunches more accessible, and factories have been established for expressing

CROP	COUNTRY	PRODUCTION	
		Peasant	Plantation
OIL PALM*	Belgian Congo	336,654 hectares	128,607 ha.
	British West Africa†	Oil 140,000	—
		Kernels 322,739	—
	French West and Equatorial Africa	Oil 38,000	—
		Kernels 130,181	—
	Angola	Oil 4,437	—
		Kernels 19,941	—
	Netherlands E.I.	—	151,000 acres
	British Malaya	—	49,455 acres

* "Survey of Vegetable Oilseeds and Oils," Vol. I, *Oil Palm Products.* E.M.B., 54, 1932. Figures of acreage are only available for the new plantation areas.

Figures of oil and kernels are for tons of exports. Statistics of production are not available for these native producing areas. "Local consumption absorbs an appreciable part of the produce." All figures are for 1930. Plantation production has rapidly increased in the last decade; since the fall in price in 1929, native African has shown a tendency to decline.

† About 95 per cent of the exports from these areas come from Nigeria.

the oil. The tree has also been introduced into Malaya and Sumatra by plantations, and production in these countries has rapidly increased.

The controlling factor in palm-oil production is that the pericarp which yields the oil must be crushed immediately after the fruit is cut, and the factory can obtain a larger return of oil and also maintain a higher quality than the native crusher, whose methods produce a large proportion of free fatty acid which reduces the market value of the oil. The kernels can be shipped without deterioration, but their market value follows that of coconut oil, for which palm-kernel oil is in many respects a substitute, and they are not so valuable as the oil of the pericarp. The future of the native industry in competition with plantations seems to depend either on the invention of a small individual crusher as efficient as factory methods or on the formation of co-operative factories by native producers. The factories which have been established on concessions in the African palm belt are very much dependent on native labour in order to maintain supplies of fruit, and it ought to be possible to introduce some scheme of co-operation between labourers and factories similar to those which have been found successful in the sugar-cane and cotton industries.

As a cultivated crop rubber is hardly out of the experimental stage. The substance first became of importance in commerce as a wild forest product, but this has been virtually eliminated from the market by the enormous success of the cultivated tree, *hevea brasiliensis*, in regions where it has been acclimatized. Although not indigenous to Malaya and the East Indies, the tree has been cultivated as extensively by natives as by foreign estates, and there was a continuous increase of acreage until the collapse of price in 1929. Constant improvements in the methods of tapping and treating the rubber have brought about appreciable reductions in the cost of production, and a great deal has been learnt about preserving the health of the tree and increasing its yield. The industry has many features which would seem to mark it out for organization on a highly capitalized scale. There are several years of waiting before the trees can be tapped, then they occupy the land to the exclusion of other crops for a very long period, so that the area of revenue and food cultivation cannot be changed when prices fluctuate; the machinery for rolling and drying the latex has become expensive and elaborate, so that the native does not receive as high a price as the plantation for the product he prepares himself; and, moreover, the industry has developed in areas where it could obtain adequate supplies of hired labour. Nevertheless, the competition of the native product with the European continues to be the chief problem of the industry. In proximity to the estates

CROP	COUNTRY	ACREAGE	
		Peasant	Plantation
RUBBER*	Netherlands E.I.	1,815,000	1,439,000
	Malaya	1,220,000	1,853,000
	Ceylon	184,000	362,000
	British Borneo	310,000	84,000
	Indo-China	—	280,000
	Siam	150,000	—
	Others	—	75,000

* Figures are from the *Bulletin of the Rubber Growers' Association*, April 1933, and refer to the acreage at December 31, 1931. It should be noted that both peasants and plantations grow what is commercially designated as "plantation rubber" in order to distinguish it from the wild forest product. Hence large cultivated holdings are usually referred to as "estates."

are large numbers of native landowners who prefer cultivating their own land to working for wages; these have been helped by the Government with seedlings and advice, and they can sell their product either in the raw state to a factory or crudely prepared to a merchant. Although it brings a lower price than the estate product, they seem to prefer it to any other crop they might cultivate.

Sugar-cane is grown for internal consumption in practically every part of the tropics. The few areas that grow primarily for export purposes—Cuba, the Netherlands

Indies, Hawaii, the Philippines, Peru, and the West Indies—are distinguished from the others by their large-scale cultivation units, their extensive mechanical equipment and their

CROP	COUNTRY	ACREAGE	
		Peasant	Plantation
SUGAR-CANE*	Brazil	—	1,210,000
	British Guiana	—	61,000
	Colombia	—	270,000
	Peru	—	100,000
	British West Indies	—	162,000†
	French West Indies	—	40,000
	Cuba	—	2,700,000‡
	Porto Rico	—	200,000
	India	2,855,000§	—
	Netherlands E.I.	26,000	412,000
	Philippines	175,000	465,000
	Fiji	—	39,055
	Hawaii	—	340,000
	Mauritius	—	134,915
	Kenya	—	12,363
	Uganda	—	13,246

* Figures for British colonies from *Statistical Abstract for the British Empire*. For other areas from *I.Y.A.S.*, *The Report of Proceedings of the Imperial Sugar Cane Research Conference*, London, 1931, published by the E.M.B., surveys the organization of the industry all over the world. The acreage given is for 1931, before schemes of limitation came into effect.

† A large proportion of this consists of peasant holdings whose canes are crushed by a factory.

‡ The usual *colono* holding on which canes are grown for the factories is 300 to 500 acres.

§ This comprises 95 per cent of the total area.

scientific methods at every stage of production. Both the costs and the price of the product are greatly influenced by the tariffs, subsidies, and protected markets which different

Governments have granted to their own section of the industry. But in spite of this and the widespread production of competitive beet sugar, a large international trade in cane sugar continues for two reasons. In many producing countries the domestic industry cannot meet the internal demand; and secondly, most of the sugar shipped by growers is in the form of yellow crystals, which are refined in the large industrial centres and re-exported to final consumers. The sugar-cane is in some places an annual crop, in others it grows well in rotation with food crops, but so great has been its progress under scientific management, primitive methods of production cannot compete with modern; and except when his local market is beyond the range of competition, the small cultivator now grows his canes under expert advice and supervision. The canes have to be crushed immediately after they are cut as delay diminishes the yield of juice, hence the factory must be situated in the producing district. But the processes of cultivation and sugar-making require entirely different technical management, and so a system has developed whereby large factories obtain all or part of their supplies by contract with small growers instead of undertaking direct cultivation with hired labour. In order to maintain the quality of the cane, however, these growers are supervised by the agricultural experts of either the Government or the factory. In spite of the elaborate machinery necessary for manufacturing sugar, the labour costs of cultivation and reaping remain by far the larger part of total costs, and are a higher proportion of this total for sugar-cane than for any other crop. This is the main reason why so much attention has been paid by the sugar industry to organizing its labourers by methods which give them a direct interest in final productivity, and also make them to a great extent participators in the risk of price fluctuations of the finished product. Another aspect of the matter, however, is that a large central factory does represent a considerable investment, and it is a specific factor, while the land of peasants is not, so that where factories have grown to rely on cultivating areas which they do not themselves own, it is necessary to offer the planters every inducement not to change to another crop.

CROP	COUNTRY	ACREAGE	
		Peasant	Plantation
TEA*	China†	—	—
	India	—	807,433
	Ceylon	—	400,000
	Netherlands E.I.	113,000	370,000
	Formosa	120,000	—
	Japan	95,000	—
	Nyasaland	—	11,414
	Kenya	—	11,258
	Tanganyika	—	1,100

* Figures for 1930 from *I.Y.A.S.* Restriction of the output of tea is secured, not by a reduction in acreage, but by fixing a finer pluck which takes less leaf from the shoot.

† Figures of acreage are not available, total production can only be estimated. Exports in 1930 were 405,843 quintals.

Tea had been grown by small farmers in China for centuries before traders introduced it to Europe, and exports reached as much as three hundred million pounds per year in the 1880's. Then the plantation tea that was being cultivated in Assam and Ceylon began to capture China's foreign market; and, except for exports to Russia, the Chinese share of foreign trade in the commodity is now negligible. A large quantity is still grown, however, for internal consumption. In India, on the other hand, the internal consumption is negligible, and the vast expansion in production is all for export. The cultivation and care of the bushes needs a great deal of hand-labour, and the crop is one that can be picked by women and children, therefore it is in some respects suited to peasant cultivation; but in its modern form it has been kept a plantation industry by the expensive and complex machinery required for withering, rolling, fermenting, and drying the leaf. Undoubtedly the Chinese farmer prepared his leaf with great skill, but the cost of preparing, collecting, and shipping small quantities from scattered areas could not compete with the unified production of plantations. Moreover, the peasant was dependent upon favourable

CROP	COUNTRY	ACREAGE	
		Peasant	Plantation
TOBACCO*	India	1,300,000	—
	Netherlands E.I.	446,000	140,000
	Brazil	—	250,000
	Cuba	—	150,000
	Porto Rico	—	40,000
	Philippines	190,000	—
	Mexico	35,000	—
	Ceylon	12,000	—
	Nyasaland	27,000	14,000
	Southern Rhodesia	—	28,000

* Figures for 1930 from *I.Y.A.S.*

weather conditions to obtain a good quality product. Peasant production in Formosa and Japan has been carefully organized to overcome these difficulties, and the chief product of these areas is *oolong*, a partly green tea. In the Netherlands Indies the natives sell the leaf they grow on their own land to factories for processing. The reason why similar peasant organization has not developed in India and Ceylon is that the crop is not an indigenous culture, and the tea companies obtained unoccupied lands and then imported labourers.

An important factor in the tobacco industry is the established diversity of demand for different varieties and qualities of leaf. Thus the Virginia tobacco of the United States[1] has long enjoyed a large market for which Nyasaland and Rhodesia have recently begun to compete. The plantations in the Dutch Indies cultivate for the European market, while the natives in most places in the East grow and prepare a leaf for local consumption, as do larger units of cultivation in South and Central America. Cuban farmers specialize in high-grade cigar leaf, while Philippine producers have found a large demand for aromatic cigarette tobacco.

CROP	COUNTRY	ACREAGE	
		Peasant	Plantation
GROUND-NUTS*	India	6,000,000	—
	Netherlands E.I.	250,000	—
	French West Africa	1,000,000	—
	Nigeria	1,000,000	—
	Belgian Congo	300,000	—
	Gambia	200,000	—
	French Cameroons	160,000	—
	Uganda	100,000	—

* Figures for 1931 from *I.Y.A.S.* This is so completely a native culture that the acreage is largely estimated. There is also a considerable area under the crop in China.

The groundnut is one of the ancient foods of the tropics, and has only become of significance in foreign markets comparatively recently. It is easily grown, but requires laborious picking by hand; it can be sold after harvesting without further processing, and the final feature which marks it out for native cultivation is that it keeps well, and can be transported to shipping-points without damage by primitive

[1] Over two million acres were under cultivation in 1930–31.

methods. Groundnuts are a staple food over a large part of the area where they grow, but in the foreign market they are valued for their oil, which is used as a substitute for olive oil, while the residue is made into cattle feed.

CROP	COUNTRY	ACREAGE	
		Peasant	Plantation
MAIZE*	Brazil (1928–29)	12,800,000	—
	India	6,700,000†	—
	Netherlands E.I.	3,800,000	—
	Philippines	1,300,000	—
	Indo-China	560,000	—
	Kenya (1929)	405,000	250,000
	Rest of Tropical Africa	2,000,000 (approx.)	—

* Figures for 1930 from the *I.Y.A.S.* and the *Statistical Abstract of the British Empire*. As happens with all native crops, some of the area has to be estimated. † Incomplete.

Maize is one of the chief food crops of the tropics, and is sold at most native markets. European settlers have begun to cultivate the crop for sale in a few regions of practically temperate altitude; but while it is a crop well adapted to large-scale mechanized farming, it has never been necessary to develop it by plantation methods because the supply from non-tropical regions has been ample for the requirements of international trade. The assistance of agricultural experts has brought about a marked improvement in the yield of the native crop in some places, and it has also proved suitable for rotating with cotton.

Rice is the staple foodstuff of the tropical parts of the Orient, and of some of the sub-tropical also. It has become besides an important export from some regions, mainly Burma and Siam. The trade is largely with other parts of the East, for some producing areas do not meet their internal demand, and especially with Malaya, Ceylon, and Mauritius, where enough is not grown to feed the labour that migrated from other rice-eating areas, and a small quantity is also consumed in European countries. Although some landowners hold comparatively large areas of rice land, it has remained pre-eminently an industry of

CROP	COUNTRY	ACREAGE	
		Peasant	Plantation
RICE*	India	88,400,000	—
	Burma	13,000,000	—
	Indo-China	14,000,000	—
	Java	9,200,000	—
	Siam	6,730,600	—
	Philippines	1,790,610	—
	Ceylon	885,000	—
	British Malaya	745,000	—
	British Guiana	84,000	—
	Africa	4,900,000†	—

* Figures for 1930 from *I.Y.A.S.* and *Statistical Abstract for the British Empire.* There is also a very large area under rice in China, although the extent of it is unknown; and the crop is also grown in Japan, who imports further quantities to meet the internal demand.

† Including 380,000 acres in Egypt.

small cultivators, and the yield of the crop has been greatly improved in some places by the supervision of Government experts. While it is a crop that requires industrious cultivation, often under exacting conditions, the grain keeps well after it has been harvested, and can be exported in the *padi*, which means that it needs no preparation after it has been picked. The rice intended for local consumption is usually threshed by the natives by primitive methods—an occupation for which all the members of a family are useful, but the exports to Europe are polished in mills there before reaching the final consumer. The metropolitan powers have had an interest in developing this crop because it is such an important foodstuff, and the irrigated land on which it is grown in many areas has also proved suitable for other rotation crops, but it is not a culture for which European demand has provided a stimulus.

CHAPTER IV

THE CONDITIONS OF LABOUR SUPPLY

THE demand for labour is nowhere unified or homogeneous, and the importance of the requirements of agriculture as compared with those of mining, forestry, and public works varies between different places. In Fiji and Mauritius, for example, development has been entirely agricultural; in Northern Rhodesia it is predominantly mineral; and the plantations of Nyasaland and Mozambique have to compete with the labour needs of the Rand mines. Moreover, although foreign efforts at development are primarily, and almost entirely, concerned with the cultivation and extraction of raw materials, the transport and marketing of these give rise to several subsidiary occupations; and the Government demand for labour for roads and public works is frequently a considerable factor in the market.[1] The main types of labour demand may be classified according to the nature of the employment as follows:

CONTINUOUS: for mining, to some extent for agriculture, for porterage where other means of transport is deficient, in domestic service and skilled occupations.

SEASONAL: additional agricultural labour at times of planting and harvesting, and sometimes timber-cutting.

NON-RECURRENT: for construction works, and clearing waste or forest land.

EMERGENCY: consequent on drought, flood, or famine.

Some of this labour is used directly for Government purposes, usually that for public works, roads, and to a

[1] Aileyne Ireland, *The Far Eastern Tropics*, p. 229, shows that in the Philippines the ability of the Government to pay a wage higher than that profitable to other employers deprived private industries of the best labour.

great extent porterage, but since the other industries have been introduced with the sympathy, if not the assistance of the Government, official measures for obtaining labour do not discriminate between public and private employers. The means by which a satisfactory supply of workers for all these classes of demand can be obtained has been one of the leading problems of the administration in every tropical territory. It is a problem which raises two issues: by what principle of persuasion or coercion is the distribution of indigenous labour to be controlled? Is alien immigration to be admitted when the local supply of workers is inadequate or unsuitable?

Under their customary economy natives work regularly and methodically for the attainment of recognized ends, and what we have to consider here is how the introduction of capitalistic forms of production affects their motives for working and the final ends to which their effort is directed. The scope of the market to which they have access is greatly enlarged; in place of a choice limited by direct exchange in a particular environment, indirect exchange and foreign trade bring within their reach an extended range of both consumption and production alternatives. They may satisfy their usual wants by new means or increase their scale of total wants; and the purchasing power for these new purposes must be acquired by changing their production system from direct to indirect, that is, *either by working for wages or by growing crops for sale.*

The relative advantages of these two forms of occupation depend upon how their different degrees of profitability compare with the living conditions they respectively offer. Through the superior efficiency of its equipment and organization a plantation may be able to offer a higher rate of remuneration than the native can earn by independent production; or, on the other hand, a plantation may find its overhead and management costs so high that it cannot afford to pay labour as much as a peasant can obtain by selling the produce of the same amount of time and labour expended on his own account. And besides this difference in the productivity value of his labour, another determinant in the native's choice of occupation is the difference in the conditions under which he will have to work as a wage-earner and as an independent producer. He may dislike leaving the familiar surroundings of his home to work for several months on a plantation a long distance away, or he may welcome the opportunity of travelling in new country; he may prefer the comparative freedom of working on his own land to the regular discipline of wage employment, or he may find that the plantation offsets this disadvantage by providing more attractive food and housing than his own village. We may say, therefore, that the response which an indigenous people make to the new conditions introduced by capitalism depends upon three determinants of individual motives: the need of money, which decides in the first place the extent of the effort the native will make to produce for exchange; the preference for one set of living conditions over another shown by various labourers; and the desire of some natives to travel outside their tribal area, which should probably be regarded as an initial rather than a permanent stimulus.

How these motives may combine in a particular case was seen by de Brazza's secretary in the French Congo during the scandals and atrocities of the concession regime. "Le colon, qui a besoin d'une main d'œuvre fidèle, est obligé d'attirer et de retenir ses travailleurs noirs, en les traitant bien, les nourrissant bien, et les payant bien. Ils les paye souvent en argent, et non pas seulement en marchandaises."[1] In some undeveloped districts it would be difficult for labourers to get the food they want to purchase even if they had the money, there would be no sellers; but a European

[1] F. Challaye, *Le Congo Français*, 1909, p. 166.

planter with better weapons for hunting game than native communities possess can offer the attraction of exceptional food. Challaye found one in the Congo, a "grand chasseur, a la réputation de bien nourrir ses employés noirs, qu'il attire et retient par leur désir de viande," etc.[1] And in spite of the widespread dislike of ordinary porterage, it is possible to get natives in most parts of Africa to go as porters with hunting expeditions because they expect a generous distribution of game.

Another incentive to labourers to live on plantations is found in the Edea district of the Cameroons under French mandate where chiefs are cultivating cacao and other crops on a large scale. The chief loans one of his wives to a worker who has none of his own, and who is then quite willing to stay on the plantation as he would find it difficult to obtain a wife otherwise.[2] A close parallel to this form of inducement was devised by a planter in the Congo who, "ayant vécu longtemps dans le pays, connaissant les mœurs des indigènes, les utilise à son profit: sachant que l'achat d'une femme est la grande préoccupation des Pahouins, il a acheté des femmes aux travailleurs qu'il emploie à planter des cacaoyers ou faire le commerce du bois, et il s'est acquis ainsi leur obéissance, leur concours fidèle."[3] It appears, however, to be more usual for the native to work for the money to buy a wife for himself, and this is one of the chief purposes for which he requires cash.[4]

The continuity of a labour supply curve based on the need of money depends upon that need being constant, and people accustomed to a self-sufficing economy only feel this constancy of need if they have acquired a taste for necessities which must be regularly purchased from outside. If their

[1] Idem, note.
[2] Buell, op. cit., *French Cameroons*, Vol. II, p. 346.
[3] Challaye, op. cit., p. 166, note.
[4] *E.A. Commission*, Cmd. 2387, 1925.

new tastes comprise only curiosities and occasional exceptions to their customary wants, their need of purchasing power will be correspondingly erratic and transitory. Similarly, if the members of any community are willing to make an extra effort only to obtain money for a special celebration such as a wedding, when habitual consumption goods will not suffice, or to provide new village buildings, or in order to discharge debts contracted in times of bad harvest or other misfortunes,[1] they will provide merely a discontinuous and short-term labour supply.

Not the least of the changes made by European penetration of backward areas has been the opening of means of communication between districts hitherto distinct and isolated with resultant opportunities for natives to travel in safety outside their own territory.[2] Previously the position of a traveller was dangerous as well as difficult, if he did not meet an enemy he was likely to fall into the hands of a slave-trader. Foreign intervention not only removed these dangers, but by its demand for labour from great distances it gave a positive impetus to any desire natives had to travel and see strange places. "The African native," says Major Orde Browne, "is a great traveller," and he gives an impressive description of the intercourse that goes on: "The Rand recruits largely from Portuguese East Africa, Rhodesia from Mozambique, the Belgian Congo attracts men from Angola, the French West African countries furnish a stream of travellers seeking work or markets in British territory. Eritrea draws its best labour from the Sudan, Zanzibar's cloves are picked by men from Kenya or Tanganyika, and

[1] G. T. Garratt, "The Indian Industrial Worker," *E. J.*, September 1932, says that the average worker from up-country goes to the mill area in the same spirit as a European peasant might serve his time as a conscript. Most cultivators are in debt, and they go to earn wages with the idea of freeing themselves from the moneylender.

[2] McG. Ross in *Kenya from Within*, p. 185, gives an interesting account of the early stages of this process.

so the fusion goes on."[1] Against this, however, we have the statement of a Government commission in 1889, "The native has a strong home instinct, and dislikes work at any distance from his own district,"[2] and again in 1903, "The Kavirondo and Kikuyu dislike to leave their homes even for a month, and will do no outside work at all during the season of cultivation."[3] And Lieutenant-Colonel Harding states that when he was Commissioner of Northern Rhodesia, he was averse from the recruiting of native labour for the mines of Johannesburg because of the distance, and of the reluctance of native chiefs to allow their young men to go to unknown surroundings.[4] This apparent conflict of opinion is no doubt to be explained in two ways; that there is a great difference between being forced to go long distances to perform unattractive tasks—possibly to the detriment of your own undertakings at home—and setting out on your own initiative to gain information and reap benefits in new places, and the Government inquiries found those who had gone unwillingly while Major Browne has more recently seen those who are moving about of their own free will. And secondly, that Africans, either as individuals or tribes, may not be of such identical disposition in this respect that one statement of any kind is applicable to them all. There is still a further question, however, as to whether members of different tribes would be found so widely dispersed to-day if taxation had not first made them leave home in search of work, and the answer to this will probably remain debatable.

One aspect of the matter probably worth attention is that while under the conditions of indigenous economy every

[1] Browne, op. cit., "African Labour and International Relations," *J.A.S.*, October 1932.

[2] *Report on Uganda Railway*, Cd. 9331, 1889.

[3] *Report on Slavery and Forced Labour in the British East Africa Protectorate*, Cd. 1631, 1903.

[4] Harding, Lt.-Col. C., *Far Bugles*, p. 112.

member depends for support upon his position in the community, when wage employment is introduced it offers an alternative means of subsistence to the communal resources, and so provides an opportunity of escape for any natives who dislike their position and obligations in the tribe. A small number are found in towns everywhere who prefer the greater freedom of living there on their own initiative to the limitations and restrictions of life in their original village. They may be said to have exchanged the security offered by the established system of tribal economy for the risk of undefined gains under the new conditions of life, and their number is growing; for when a man has learnt the money value of his labour he is unwilling to work at the unpaid obligations of tribal life.[1] But while this attitude is responsible for a large proportion of the detribalized natives in urban centres, and is an important factor in maintaining a voluntary labour supply for artisan and mechanical occupations, it has little effect upon agricultural labour. The detribalized class of squatters has been created by the shortage of lands of their own consequent upon large concessions to foreigners in their territory.[2]

At the present time the attitude of indigenous tropical peoples to labour under foreign stimulus is not everywhere the same. Some have been familiar with capitalistic economy longer than others; the natural resources of various regions differ greatly, with a consequent variety of opportunities for employment; and the experience of different tribes and communities of foreign contacts has differed widely, leaving a corresponding difference of effect upon the native attitude

[1] Schapera, "Labour Migration from Bechuanaland," *J.A.S.*, October 1933, gives some examples of this.

[2] This is forcibly stated by L. S. B. Leakey in "Some Aspects of the Black and White Problem in Kenya," *Bull. of the John Rylands Library*, Vol. XV, No. 2: "Except for a very few, they [the squatters] are natives who were rendered homeless by the ignorance of those who had the control of the alienation of land to Europeans for farms."

to employment. Thus the response to foreign efforts at development now includes the repugnance to settled labour of a pastoral tribe such as the Masai; the dislike of people who have experienced slavery for labour under a master; the indifference to improved production of such fortunately situated races as the Fijians and Papuans; the preference of Singalese and Chinese for working independently; the willingness of Indians to leave their villages in order to earn more money; the transformation of hitherto belligerent tribes like the Ashantis into revenue producers; the eagerness of newly instructed people like the Baganda to grow market crops; and the readiness of others who have become congested on their resources, as in Java, to profit by co-operation with European capital.

Most widespread probably are those peoples whose attitude to working for a master has been conditioned by recent enslavement, and who regard wage employment with the same aversion as slavery. These are found as a result of Arab conquests on the East Coast of Africa, in other parts of Africa where weak tribes were enslaved by strong, and in large areas of the Orient, where previous to its abolition under European pressure in the late nineteenth century caste slavery was an integral part of the social system.[1] Not only are these people reluctant to enter employment, but they usually show little enterprise on their own account, the legacy of a slave regime seems to be complete apathy to self-improvement. The second type of labour, almost as inaccessible to employers, but for a different reason, are those tribes accustomed to a self-sufficing economy who have as yet had no experience of foreign contacts, and are indifferent to earning wages although they have no acquired

[1] This situation in Africa is discussed by Orde Browne, op. cit., p. 27. Knowles, op. cit., p. 174, mentions a similar labour difficulty in Malaya and Assam. W. L. Mathieson, in *British Slavery and its Abolition*, and *British Slave Emancipation*, deals with the labour situation that followed abolition in the British West Indies.

prejudice against it. These are found most notably in the Pacific archipelago, but comprise also those tribes of interior Africa who have been untouched by foreign trade or invasion. Having no need for money, they think it unnecessary to exert themselves to earn any, and their interest in development depends upon their growing consciousness of this need. Thirdly, there is the class of labour which comes predominantly from the crowded areas of India and China, which is accustomed to an exchange economy and willing to work to meet its need of money. These people have for the most part a shrewder bargaining capacity than the others, they estimate the monetary attractions of different occupations more readily, and are usually even more anxious to undertake production of their own than to enter paid employment. In this class also are those peasants and traders of West Africa who have rapidly adapted their economy to the requirements and opportunities of foreign commerce. These had, of course, for long been in contact with the Mediterranean world through the Arab trade routes of Northern Africa, but the pressure of population on the land had not become great enough to make the struggle for a livelihood as severe as it was in the Orient.

But whatever may be the forces that influence the native's wants they determine his motives for working, and the distribution of his effort under changing conditions of labour is guided by the extent to which new wants are substituted for old in his scale of preferences. The marginal calculation which he has to make is whether a paid occupation with all that it implies of innovation and onerousness is worth the benefits to be derived from having the additional purchasing-power, a choice that was clearly stated by the Tahitians in 1823 in their reply to a foreign offer of a higher standard of living, "We should like some of these things very well, but we cannot have them without working; that we do not like, and therefore would rather do without them."[1]

Foreign landowners have held the opinion that even when the natives did decide to work for additional purchasing power, if they were enabled to become producers on their own account labour would not be obtainable for large-scale undertakings, and most territories have been developed on the basis of either plantation or peasant production.[2] It is now claimed, however, to be a wrong assumption that independent production will prevent the natives taking wage-earning employment. "Instances are frequent," says Major Orde Browne, "where natives will plant a crop intended for sale, go away to work for a while, and return to market their produce."[3] And Sir Hubert Murray thinks that the establishment of native plantations in Papua has not affected the supply of labour for other employment.[4] It would look from this as though the inculcation of the habit of exchange production did not merely bring about a change in the application of effort, but also augmented the total expenditure of effort, a situation which shows that the demand for money is elastic. In contrast with this, however, are conditions in Malaya, Ceylon, and Fiji, where the plantation demand for labour has been met by immigration, while native peasants continue to cultivate both

[1] Roberts, *Population Problems of the Pacific*, p. 207.

[2] C. A. Barber, *Modern Agricultural Research in the Empire*, E.M.B., 2, points out that in British Colonies Government assistance has usually been confined to European agriculture, and gives the example of Ceylon, where, until very recently, no attention was paid to the peasant, while in India, in the absence of European undertakings, the peasant has always received assistance. In Kenya, at the present time, there is less revenue production on the part of natives than in the neighbouring protectorates. The development of French West Africa has been predominantly peasant, while that of Equatorial Africa was concessionaire.

[3] Op. cit., p. 44. And the Economic and Finance Comm., Kenya, 1922, reported that "as native production increased, so did the labour supply."

[4] Op. cit., p. 273.

food and revenue crops on their own land. If the native's demand schedule expands with the new opportunities of spending, the extent to which he can satisfy his wants by independent production depends upon the area of his land and the proportion of it he can give to money instead of food crops. In Java, excessive subdivision has made most individual holdings unremunerative in comparison with plantation employment,[1] but in Malaya there is not yet this stimulus to wage-earning. In some parts of Africa the native's revenue crop is rather exiguous[2] although the land available is comparatively extensive, while in Kenya cultivable land in the native reserves is distinctly limited. Under these conditions the native may well find it necessary to meet his monetary needs by plantation employment, but in Fiji he enjoys not only a restful indifference to pressing needs of cash, but an ample supply of land for all his wants.

However much the tastes of native peoples may change, and their standard of living rise, as long as they remain in possession of their own lands they will not form a supply of wage labour on the same basis as a proletariat. At every stage of their moving demand curve they will have a choice between tribal and extra-tribal, independent production and wage-earning, means of satisfying their wants. If the choice they make excludes foreign employment, or accepts it only at a rate which the productivity value of their labour does not warrant, then, if that foreign enterprise is to be carried on, the problem arises of devising expedients which will make the supply of labour conform to the requirements of employers. And just as in indigenous society "agrarian conditions and the social structure form one indivisible

[1] G. Gongripp, "Economic Position of the Indigenous Population of the Netherlands East Indies," *Asiatic Review*, January 1927.

[2] Some of the cotton plots in Uganda, for instance, are only ¼ acre, and 12,500 native growers in Kilimanjaro exported 7,100 tons of coffee in 1932.

whole" because the economic and political systems are co-ordinated, in the same way when foreign penetration begins the Government decides the particular industrial system which is to be established, and frames its policy in support of it.

Broadly stated, the choice of the administration lies between coercion and inducement, and although slavery has now been repudiated as an instrument of labour by the metropolitan powers, it has played such an important part in tropical development that we may still make a short examination of its significance as a factor of production before considering the contemporary methods of obtaining a labour supply.

When a production system is based on slavery it means that the employer has made a capital investment in labour; and he fixes its standard of living according to his conception of maintenance costs. The labourer has no choice and no alternatives, and only the imminence of penalties stimulates his exertions.[1] The precise nature of the conditions responsible for slavery—whether it was the outcome of military operations[2] or was due to the absence of a circulating wage fund for labour,[3] as has been variously suggested—are not relevant to the aspect of the system we want to consider here, which is only that of the relationship of employers to workers whom they own. A slave economy rests entirely on the owners' decisions as to the distribution of labour. They dispose of the worker's time

[1] A. E. Zimmern in *Was the Greek City State Founded on Slavery?* discusses the incentive of earning freedom as a necessary element in the high degree of skill shown by the slaves employed in the arts in Greece. When the type of work required necessitates this incentive, the worker is more of an apprentice than a slave. But in the tropical colonies of modern times this situation only arose with regard to a small number of artisan slaves who were allowed to buy their freedom with their earnings.

[2] J. K. Ingram, *History of Slavery.*

[3] Hunter, *Annals of Rural Bengal,* quoted Knowles, op. cit., p. 173.

and endeavour to ensure his effort also. It is indeed the distinguishing characteristic of slave labour that it is always directed to the ends of a master, and the worker never has the opportunity of serving ends of his own. The Slavery Convention of the League of Nations defined slavery as "the status or condition of a person over whom any or all of the powers attaching to the right of ownership are exercised,"[1] and the laws of different countries attach various powers to this right. Roman law recognized slavery as a human status and the slave as personal property, over whom an owner had more restricted rights than could be exercised over real property; and whenever the laws of modern imperial nations have been based on the Roman code, they have recognized this distinction and protected certain personal rights of the slave.[2] In a somewhat similar manner the Koran enjoins humane treatment of the slaves of a household both in their prime and in old age. But the English Common Law was in its origins unacquainted with the personal status of slavery, and when it was called on to define the position of people who were in fact slaves, it classed them with real property. They were chattels with none of the rights against the absolute power of a master which the Roman law recognized.[3]

The legal abolition of slavery by the European Powers,[4] of course, removed all the significance of these basic laws—except so far as Moslems who continue to own slaves are

[1] League of Nations Publications, C.586, M.223, 1926.

[2] Sir H. Maine, *Ancient Law*, p. 180, "Wherever servitude is sanctioned by institutions which have been deeply affected by Roman jurisprudence, the servile condition is never intolerably wretched."

[3] Maine, op. cit., says, "the English Common Law, as recently interpreted, has no true place for the slave, and can only, therefore, regard him as a chattel." In British Colonies slaves were bought and sold without regard to their family relationship or established residence.

[4] Dates of abolition: Britain, 1834; France, 1848; Holland, 1863; United States, 1865; Cuba, 1870; Portugal, 1878; Brazil, 1888.

bound by the Koran.[1] It put the system of production on a new basis, for it meant that the employer now had to obtain labour without owning the person of the labourer. But did this change in status that denied rights of ownership prevent the exercise of all the powers that had previously attached to that right? When we consider the methods of organizing labour which have superseded legal slavery in tropical territories, it will be useful to remember that the fundamental test of a free economy is whether the worker serves his own ends by his labour. It is characteristic of the roundabout system of production that he serves somebody else's ends immediately as the means of serving his own ends ultimately;[2] and this is what backward people do if they elect to work for money instead of continuing their customary hand-to-mouth production. But if their change to new occupations does not represent a voluntary choice on their own part, the fact that they are paid for their labour does not mean that they are free workers.[3]

When ownership of the person of the worker is excluded there remains, in general, two methods of obtaining a labour supply from a self-sufficing community, and both show modifications and differences of detail in the various places where they are used. One method is to UNDERMINE THE NATIVES' INDEPENDENCE by removing their sources of subsistence other than foreign employment and means in practice restricting the land to which they have free access. Then they must either earn wages or pay a labour rent to the new landowner. It is administratively possible to

[1] Orde Browne, op. cit., p. 15, says that Arabs in East Africa did not take advantage of the declaration of freedom by the British Government to turn adrift the old slaves they had been supporting.

[2] Wicksteed, *Commonsense of Political Economy*, p. 168, states this elementary point very clearly; it has tended to be obscured by the greater pertinacity of the doctrine of proletarian wage-slavery.

[3] We exclude, that is to say, the Rousseauistic hypothesis that they must be forced to be free for the social good.

enforce such a system only in comparatively small areas such as Guatemala where the confiscation of land created a class of peons, and in areas where there is extensive European settlement such as South Africa and Kenya where the shortage of their own land makes natives into squatters on white farms. The other method is to IMPOSE NEW OBLIGATIONS and CREATE NEW DESIRES for which the old resources are inadequate, and this is done in several ways.

1. The customary economy may be broken down without the use of money. Unpaid labour is exacted in the form of a labour tax, of which the *prestation* of France and the *heerendienst* of the Dutch East Indies are notable examples; or where the support of the chief is secured, he can be made to call out tribal labour for the new purposes of the metropolitan government.

2. Native society may be assimilated to the foreign system of money exchange. This is the end pursued by those countries which aim at making their dependencies into markets for manufactures as well as sources of raw materials. Here again there are two alternatives: (*a*) a policy of ECONOMIC INDUCEMENT—that is, of expanding the native consciousness of wants or making their demand schedule more elastic, or by offering working conditions under wage employment more attractive than those of the native village. (*b*) SUBSTITUTES FOR ECONOMIC INDUCEMENT, which are administrative devices for making the natives find it necessary to undertake additional labour. (i) Levying a money tax forces them either to sell produce or earn wages, and was a popular policy of pioneer administration in the nineteenth century, especially in the British colonies. (ii) A certain amount of cultivation over and above their customary level can be made compulsory and the surplus marketed by the Government. This method has recently been applied in Papua and the Belgian Congo where land is plentiful and cultivation standards low. (iii) Direct pres-

sure may be exerted to make the natives gather produce for the concessionaire of their district and an arbitrary wage paid to avoid the designation of "forced labour." This situation is always likely to arise where the voluntary response of the natives to low remuneration is slow, and political authority is in favour of rapid development. Thus it was frequent in the large conceded areas of the Congo.

Since the form of native employment as well as the methods of obtaining a labour supply are determined by Government policy, the course of economic development really depends in the ultimate analysis upon the forces and conditions that influence the Government. In many places these conditions, and the forces they generate, arose before there was a clear conception of either a labour problem or governmental responsibility for a native population; thus it was the suitability of the climate that made South Africa predominantly a white man's land, while opposite climatic factors retained the Gold Coast for African development. In other places local policy has been largely determined by theories applied from outside; this has been characteristic especially of the modern French colonies.[1] But the Portuguese and the Spanish, and the Dutch after them, established their early colonies with a distinctly predetermined idea of the purpose to which they were to conform. As a result of varied theories and historical influences and contemporary conditions, the political regulation of labour in each territory is at the present time based on the particular theory of inter-racial relationship, commonly called "the Native's place," which prevails there. A wide variation of policies between different nationalities and areas can be traced to four distinct theories of this sort.

1. That it is the native's place to be an inferior labouring

[1] Roberts, *History of French Colonial Policy*, Chap. XVII, "A Comparative Study," suggests that while French policy was dogmatic, English was pragmatic.

class for advancing civilization; which is the predominant doctrine of settlers in areas of European colonization, notably South Africa and Kenya, and is in principle comparable to the old Spanish policy in America.

2. That the native is *un attardé* who, by contact and education, can eventually be assimilated to European standards of culture, but until then he has no political rights. This has been the dominant theory of French colonization, and is generally known as the "Latin doctrine."

3. That the native is an independent worker, free to meet the new economic conditions on the same terms as Europeans. In principle this policy applies to both the labour and the land of the native, but in practice there is no real competition between European and native labour in tropical countries, and as native freedom is restricted in non-tropical, it is, for practical purposes, to the ownership and use of land that the policy of free bargaining applies, in Malaya, Ceylon, and the Philippines.

4. That the native is material for a civilization *sui generis*, and must be protected from the destructive influences of European pressure while he develops along hereditary lines. This is the basic theory of government in British West Africa, in Uganda, and of the League of Nations Mandates.

In addition to all these forms of relationship between indigenous peoples and Europeans, there is also in every tropical dependency the further problem of the position of Oriental immigrants or "cheap labour." It was pointed out in the previous chapter that a great density and consequent low productivity of labour is characteristic of Oriental economy, and hence for a very large number of people employment by foreign capital is more remunerative than their traditional local occupations. The Chinese migrated originally to islands in the Pacific; later they were taken to Malaya, Mauritius, British Guiana, and eventually the Transvaal; and economic development has attracted increasing numbers to the Netherlands Indies, Ceylon, and Indo-China.[1] After the abolition of negro slavery, Indian coolies were recruited for agricultural labour in the West Indies, British Guiana, Fiji, Mauritius, and Natal, and large numbers still move freely between the mainland and Ceylon and Malaya.[2] The Hawaiian Islands were developed largely by Japanese and Chinese labour, and in recent years France has recruited Annamites for labour in her under-populated Pacific territory.[3] That both Indians and Chinese are not found in still larger numbers in foreign countries is due to political regulations, and not to the cessation of economic inducement.

These races have been excluded from non-tropical regions because they were regarded as detrimental to the European standard of living, but for the tropics where the white race cannot undertake heavy labour, they should at first sight appear to be the very alternative to unwilling and inefficient native labour which employers need, and this was indeed the view that led to the large movements of indentured coolies in the late nineteenth century. But gradually other aspects of the matter than that of cheap labour came to be considered. For the metropolitan governments, Chinese and Indian immigrants added another element to an already complicated racial situation; thus the United States found it necessary to declare that all Orientals born in Hawaii were United States citizens; and having assumed the protectorate over the territory of New Guinea in order to prevent it becoming a Japanese area, Australia has retained

[1] H. F. MacNair, *The Chinese Abroad*, 1925. Persia Campbell, *Chinese Coolie Migration to Places within the British Empire.*

[2] "Indians Overseas," *Indian Yearbook*, 1932, p. 895. Ceylon, 800,000; Malaya, 628,000, Mauritius, 229,000; Trinidad, 133,000; British Guiana, 130,000; Fiji, 75,000; Kenya, 27,000; Tanganyika, 18,000; Zanzibar, 18,000; Jamaica, 17,000; Uganda, 12,000. Of a total of 2,407,825 overseas, 2,307,350 were in the British Empire.

[3] Roberts, *Population Problems of the Pacific*, 1927, p. 244.

there the same immigration restrictions as apply in the Commonwealth,[1] although the presence of Oriental labourers and traders would undoubtedly have given an impetus to the development of the territory which has been distinctly lacking in the aboriginal inhabitants. Similarly, the United States has preferred to exclude Chinese from the Philippines and face a scarcity of labour than to compete with the plantation development of Malaya and the Dutch East Indies.[2] The sugar industry of Natal was built up with immigrant Indian labour, but when the Indians spread to other occupations and became themselves landowners, the European population protested against their presence.

Most Oriental peoples appear to have acquired from the economic exigencies of their racial history not only the ability to sustain industrious activity on very low standards of nutrition, but also a commercial shrewdness and bargaining capacity which makes them the successful rivals of almost every other race in shopkeeping and small business undertakings. Some who managed to acquire capital have proved very successful in large-scale business also; but it is especially their capacity for profiting from small resources, for acquiring property by the exercise of industry and thrift, that has made other races apprehensive of the effects of unregulated Oriental competition.[3] In contrast with these characteristics of the Chinese merchant and market-gardener, and the Indian trader and moneylender, is the lack of business shrewdness in most of the island aborigines of the Pacific, and the consequent likelihood of their becoming the victims of their bargains. Hence, where it is the policy of

[1] Sir H. Murray, *Papua of To-day*, Chap. V.

[2] L. P. Hammond, *A Survey of Economic Conditions in the Philippine Islands*, 1928.

[3] Sir H. Bell, *Foreign Colonial Administration in the Far East*, p. 216, gives expression significant of the prevailing political attitude to this question when he says, "The stealthy muffled spread of the Chinese all through South-East Asia is steadily attaining portentous proportions."

the metropolitan government to confirm natives in the ownership of their customary land, it has been as necessary to prevent it falling into the hands of pawnbrokers and moneylenders or immigrant cultivators as to refuse concessions to Europeans. In Java the native peasant may not part with the title to his land, and the Government has established pawnshops in the villages; while in Fiji, although most of the small cultivators are Indian, they lease the land from the natives under Government supervision.[1] In contrast with this situation, we find in Mauritius, where there were no aboriginal interests to be protected, that the Indians who went in originally as plantation labour under the same conditions as they went to Fiji, now own about half the cultivated area.[2] In British West Africa native land policy excludes the alienation of land for any kind of foreign settlement, but although the other Powers have been willing to grant European concessions in the West African territories, they have not permitted Oriental immigration. And besides the diplomatic attitude of the Imperial Government and the economic objections of the local community, the final factor in restricting the movement of Oriental migration to meet demands for cheap labour was the action of the emigrants' Governments. Japan and China agreed to prevent their nationals going to places where it was known that they were not wanted, and the Government of India in 1917 put an end to the whole system of indentured Indian labour, and carefully prescribed the conditions on which future labour for foreign countries should be recruited. The consequence was that while Indian coolies still went in increasing numbers to Ceylon and Malaya, their migration to Fiji, Mauritius, the West Indies, and British Guiana ceased.

In estimating the effect of immigrant labour in response

[1] A. A. Wright, *Colony of Fiji*, Suva, 1932.
[2] Mauritius, Census, 1931.

to a rate of inducement which is profitable to the employer as an alternative to persuading or coercing natives who do not voluntarily respond to such a rate, we may say that at the present time it is an essential factor in the plantation industries of Ceylon and Malaya, that after the abolition of slavery it was of great importance in maintaining plantation cultivation in Trinidad, British Guiana, and Mauritius, and subsequently formed the basis of prosperous peasant settlement in these colonies and in Fiji. In subtropical areas of European settlement, e.g. Natal and Kenya, the political aspects of the race problem seem to overshadow the financial; and the tropical areas of Africa have not been affected by the movement. Similarly, Government policy over a large area of the Pacific, e.g. Papua, the Philippines, Borneo, prevents employers from having recourse to immigrant labour, and makes local development depend upon the native inhabitants.

It is in the light of these territorially distinct racial theories of employment that we must now examine the actual measures for regulating the supply of labour which are in force in various areas. The first group of these belong to the category which we described above as *destructive of the basis of native independence*. The outright annexation of all land over which they claimed jurisdiction was the original method of colonization by the European Powers, and in so far as they were able to implement their claims they struck at the roots of the independence of the indigenous race, whether these were enslaved outright as the Indians of America were by the Spaniards or merely subjected to levies as the Javanese were by the Dutch. This latter nation has indeed surpassed all others in the simplicity of the methods with which it has directed native labour into desired channels by the removal of alternatives. When the Dutch first established trade relations with the "Spice Islands" they secured a monopoly of the export of spices by destroying all the native trees on the islands which they did not want or could not control;[1] and when they found the natives in Suriname unmindful of the need of working for a living, they cut down the banana trees which were the source of this independence.[2]

But in other tropical territories in more recent times physical conditions have prevented the imperial Power from establishing such complete and stringent control. The ends of modern colonial development are, moreover, different from those of the Spaniards, and a small area efficiently worked is of more benefit than a large one which is only managed with uncertainty and difficulty. Land tenure is still, however, the basis of administrative policy, and there are two distinct and opposite theories of native land rights in operation. One is seen in Nigeria, the Gold Coast, and Sierra Leone Protectorates where all the land is regarded as primarily belonging to the natives, and foreign concessions are only granted if they will not prejudice native interests. The opposite theory is held in its most absolute form by the French Government, which does not recognize that natives have a claim to any land until they have formally registered their titles. But in other areas, while the natives' rights to the land they occupied have been recognized, this has not been separated by survey from the unoccupied to which they were held to have no claim, and their tenure has not always proved secure.

For practical purposes the treatment of land over which the metropolitan power assumes ownership takes two forms.[3]

[1] Sir W. Foster, *England's Quest of Eastern Trade*, p. 276. Redgrove, op. cit., p. 283.

[2] Knowles, op. cit., p. 178, note.

[3] We are not dealing here with areas of European farming outside the tropics such as South Africa, or the French policy of "refoulement" in North Africa and New Caledonia, but marked similarities will be found between these and such highland areas as Kenya and Katanga, where European interests have been treated as predominant.

In the French and Belgian Congo, and in Portuguese Africa, foreign concessions are granted over wide areas without any reciprocal demarcation of areas for native use, so that the foreign holder virtually obtains also a concession over the people he finds on his land. In the British territories other than West African exclusive native rights have not been recognized, but, except in Nyasaland, definitive areas were set aside for native occupation as "Native Reserves," and the other lands passed to the Crown for alienation to non-natives.[1] In Nyasaland Europeans obtained large grants of land from native chiefs before the imperial Government took over control, and the people who were living on the land then had to pay rent in the form of labour dues.[2] It was a situation against which a tide of native resentment steadily grew and culminated in 1915 in the Chilembwe Rising. As a result of this, the Government ordered the introduction of cash rents, but in so far as the natives could find the money for these the arrangement did not suit the planters who wanted labour and not cash, and in so far as they could not find the money it did not suit the natives who disliked spending their time on plantation labour with what they regarded as insufficient pay and bad treatment. The incident is a very clear example of the way in which the landlessness of natives creates a supply of wage labour, but a long-run view must also take notice of the difficulty which plantations in Nyasaland have found in competing with peasant production of the same crops.[3]

[1] For figures of concessions and reserves in the various territories, see Appendix B.

[2] Compare this with D. M. Goodfellow, *A Modern Economic History of South Africa*, chapter on Early Native Economic Policy, p. 62, where he shows that after the first European land grants, tribal life continued by paying rent to the farmers. Later, by going to work in towns or mines, the young men could pay the rent of their families who were living outside reserves.

[3] See the previous chapter, sections on Cotton and Tobacco, for details of this. It is worth noting in this connection that a Report to

When concessions are granted without segregating the natives in other districts, and this has been the more widespread practice, the land, and with it his means of livelihood, is cut from under the native's feet. If he cannot move elsewhere, he must henceforth live—and work—on the conditions the landowners offer. He is in a similar position if for any reason—overcrowding, absence that has forfeited his claim, or tribal disagreements—he cannot live in one of the appointed native reserves and must seek a living on foreign-owned land. Where settlers are farming their grants these landless natives become squatters, growing food for themselves and paying rent to the landlord in the form of labour on his farm which may amount to one hundred and eighty days' work in the year.

In the Congo, however, the concessionaires were not concerned with cultivation, but with the extraction of wild products; and their aim was in the first place that the natives should gather these products regularly, and secondly that the price should be kept as low as possible by excluding the competition of other buyers. It was a purpose for which the Governments concerned made every effort to provide. In 1889 forty companies were granted concessions that amounted to one-third of the total area of French Congo,

the local legislature in 1933 (Sessional Paper 1), found that the natives preferred growing tobacco on Crown land to being tenant farmers on private estates. The Government appears to have decided now to apply to Nyasaland—as far as existing concessions make possible—the principles of native land rights which are in force in West Africa. Cf. Statement of the Governor to the Chiefs on the King's Birthday, 1933. *J.A.S.*, December 1933: "You will see that the King in England has decided to give you a large share in managing your own affairs. . . . He has decided that all the land in Nyasaland which is not actually used by the Government and does not already belong to people who are not natives shall not in future be sold or leased in the ordinary way. . . . The same refers to such land in N. Nyasa as may be relinquished by the B.S.A. Co. in deference to native claims." The concession on which the Chilembwe Rising centred was a single holding of nearly 300 square miles.

and over this area they were empowered to *exercer tous les droits de jouissance et d'exploitation*, while natives were prohibited from selling produce gathered in that area to traders. In order that this prohibition should not reduce productivity, a head tax payable in produce was imposed and fixed at three francs per annum, but actually the natives were made to hand over produce of a much higher market value. And in spite of many protests and disturbances it was not until 1909 that a money tax was substituted.[1]

During the Congo Free State regime native land rights were in practice ignored, and subsequent recognition of them has stopped short of delimiting specific areas. Until the collapse of the rubber boom in 1911 all the coercive resources at the disposal of both officials and concessionaires were directed to extracting rubber and ivory at the lowest possible cost to themselves. A later method of maintaining production has been that of "Tribal Contract," by which natives gathered produce—palm oil gradually became more important than rubber—both on their own land and on the surrounding concession, and sold it all exclusively to the concessionaire, which meant that the price could be fixed below what the current market value justified.[2]

It was not any imperial *de jure* change in their title to land which directly affected the economy of the natives, but the new forces of production which this change set in

[1] Buell, op. cit., Vol. II, p. 26. Ref. *Rapport d'Ensemble sur les Operations des Sociétés Concessionaires*, 1899–1904. All these concessions lapsed by 1929, and only two were renewed—Cie française du Haut Congo and la Société l'Alimaienne. The natives are now permitted to trade their produce freely, and "Bien plus, la Cie prend l'engagement de leur payer ces produits, sur toute l'étendue des territoires des anciennes concessions, à des prix fixés par l'Administration elle-même." *Y.C.C.D.*, 1930, p. 297. In view of the relations between officials and the Cie Forestière, which Gide had found a short time previously, op. cit., pp. 70–8, it would appear doubtful that a regulation which practically invites conspiracy would invariably prove "bien plus" for the native.

[2] Buell, op. cit., Vol. II, Chap. LXXXVIII.

motion. The fact that their claims to traditional rights had been overridden could make no substantial difference as long as they continued to live on the land in their customary way. But for the purpose of capitalistic development of agriculture a continuous labour supply is of more importance than the possession of extensive areas, and in tropical regions the European settler is an employer, never a labourer. And so whether foreign grants occupied an area that was large or small in comparison with that remaining in native hands, their presence created a demand for labour which could only be met by a fundamental change in the natives' system of self-sufficing production. Thus these foreign developments have a significance in native life of far greater extent than the loss of land they represent,[1] because a relatively small change in landownership brings about a very profound change in the whole orientation of native economy.

In most of the territories with which we are dealing foreign enterprise felt the need of local labour while the natives had not been deprived of enough of their land to make them dependent upon wage employment for a livelihood,[2] and the work required from them could only be secured by imposing political obligations which made it necessary, or by creating new desires for purchasable commodities which made it voluntary. At the start the decision of the administration was nearly always in favour of im-

[1] This means the amount of alienated land to which official sanction was finally given. Before European Governments intervened in Africa and the Pacific, a crowd of polyglot adventurers had secured from the native rulers of many regions concessions, grants, and rights to the land and everything on and under it, which amounted in some instances to more than the total area of which the ruler concerned had control; in Samoa, for example, the Land Commission appointed in 1893 was presented with land claims by whites amounting to more than twice the area of the islands, and allowed only 8 per cent as valid. In a slightly lesser degree the same situation prevailed in what are now the High Commission Territories of South Africa.

[2] See Appendix B for areas of foreign concessions.

posing obligations. The reason was, of course, that a decree, with zealous settlers to assist the officials in executing it, was swift and certain, and could provide with exactitude for the existing demand. In comparison with this it was a slow and unreliable process to try to inculcate a sense of need for the fruits of augmented labour. We have seen that when European traders and employers first came in contact with tropical peoples these had self-sufficing systems of economy which they found quite satisfactory, but they were willing to obtain from the foreigners any means of satisfying their established wants more efficiently. Thus gunpowder, beads, and tobacco were readily traded—they contributed to the customary way of living, but wants which implied a change of life and habit were difficult to establish.[1] And while the native need of these trade goods was great enough to supply the early foreign demand for slaves and ivory, it was not sufficient to provide the labour requirements of a large scale cueillette or plantation system, or of the Government police and constructional work which accompanied development. It was largely this sparsity of wants shown by the natives which gave support to the opinion, "There is only one effective way of dealing with the laziness and conservatism of the natives, that is compulsion, if it is hoped to obtain results in not too long a period,"[2] and this point of view has been the mainspring of colonial policy.

[1] Mary Kingsley, *West African Studies*, p. 339, says: "There is not a single thing Europe can sell to the natives that is of the nature of a true necessity, a thing the natives must have or starve. There is but one thing that even approaches in the West African markets to what wheat is in our own—that thing is tobacco."

Similarly, an early visitor said of the Samoans: "They were so rich, and in want of so little, that they disdained our instruments of iron and stuffs, and would only have beads." La Perouse, quoted Keesing, *Modern Samoa*, p. 291.

[2] Reply of Belgium to I.L.O. questionnaire on Forced Labour, 1930. Joseph Chamberlain had told Parliament with regard to African labour

Since slavery was no longer tenable, the various methods devised for compelling natives to work became known as "forced labour." The term has been commonly applied to every type of labour that could not be regarded as enjoying the status of free contract, and so it does not connote any particular system or administrative device, but it does imply some element of compulsion. The definition recently suggested by the International Labour Office is, "All work or service which is exacted from any person under the menace of any penalty for its non-performance, and for which the worker does not offer himself voluntarily."[1] The metropolitan powers pointed out in their replies that if this type of labour was going to be suppressed, exceptions would have to be made of military, fiscal and civil obligations, and penal service.[2]

The Temporary Slavery Commission appointed by the League of Nations in 1925 had found that "Corvées, unremunerated; and levies, remunerated; seem to have been recognized by every people and at every time,"[3] and it is by manipulation of tax-gathering powers old and new, supported by its police power, that imperial Government has secured most labour in Africa. Taxation may take the form of labour services when these are directly required; or a money tax may be imposed for the purpose of making

in 1898: "I think something in the nature of inducement, stimulus, or pressure is absolutely necessary if you are to secure a result which is desirable in the interests of humanity and civilization." Quoted Knowles, op. cit., p. 176.

[1] I.L.O. Convention on Forced Labour, 1930.

[2] The specific exceptions made by the respective powers are a significant index to their policies: *Belgium*: military, penal, civil and fiscal. *France:* fiscal, military, and penal. *Great Britain:* military and penal. *The Netherlands* argued that "suppression of forced labour is not yet practicable." *Portugal* thought she had already done all that was desirable or possible by her Convention of 1926, and that this proposal was "not in harmony with the dignity and rights of the State."

[3] Temporary Slavery Commission, L. of N. Documents, A.19, 1925.

the natives earn the cash for paying it. "The system of compulsory labour commutable by money payment has been introduced into several African colonies and mandated territories, such as the part of the Cameroons and of Togoland under French mandate. In other mandated territories, such as Tanganyika, Ruanda-Urundi, and part of New Guinea, the opposite system is in force. In certain cases the taxpayer can pay off the whole or part of his tax in the form of labour."[1] This system of compulsory labour France claims to be merely an extension to her colonies of the *prestations* to which citizens at home are liable, and which in "French law are exclusively considered as taxes in kind which are capable of being commuted."[2] The basis for the opposite system which does not permit the tax to be discharged in money is said by the Netherlands to be that labour dues are necessary in the Indies "to secure labour from those who have not the money to pay taxes as well as from those who would pay the taxes and leave the labour undone."[3] Belgium also was of the opinion that it was in the absence of voluntary labour that civil or fiscal obligations should be used to secure labour for "public works of general and local importance."[4]

All French subjects[5] in the colonies, but not in the mandated territories, are liable for conscription for military service, and in the Belgian Congo recruits have to be obtained for the Force Publique of sixteen thousand. In 1926 the requirements for military and ordinary labour service in French West Africa were combined by instituting a

[1] Temporary Slavery Commission, L. of N. Documents. A.19, 1925, Chap. VII, Compulsory Labour.

[2] I.L.O. Report, cit. supra.

[3] Ibid., p. 51.

[4] Ibid., p. 48.

[5] Subjects are those natives who do not qualify by assimilation to be "citizens." Hence with the exception of a few thousands all those outside the Anciennes Colonies and the original communes of Dakar are of this status, that is, the great bulk of Africans and Indonesians.

system of "Contingents Indigènes," which is virtually a Labour Army. The annual army conscripts were divided into two classes, and those in the lower class, instead of undergoing training, were made available for general works of economic development. Conscription is an important factor in the labour situation, not only when it is used to provide industrial workers, but especially when it constitutes a dominant element of competition for an already scarce supply of labour. A strangely reverse effect was noticed by Gide at one place in the Congo where natives were willing to work for less than a franc per day in order to escape being requisitioned by the administration.[1] When political obligations become so intolerable, however, they are likely to lead to migration of the population, and in the French territories of West Africa there is a law forbidding the natives to cross the boundaries because the comparative absence of coercive measures in British territories was thought to be proving too attractive to some of them. In spite of this the foreign-born Africans in the Gold Coast and Nigeria showed a marked increase in the census of 1931.

It was customary in most native tribes for the roads, bridges, and communal buildings to be kept in order by communal labour, which was summoned for the purpose by the chief at certain times of the year; and imperial Governments have eagerly made use of this custom in securing labour for roads and works on the more elaborate scale which they thought necessary. But on this scale the custom can easily become an oppressive burden, and men have been called out to work on roads when they were needed for their own crops, and women have been made to work on roads when the men had been drafted to plantations. It is to combat this kind of expedient that the Draft

[1] Gide, *Travels in the Congo*, p. 78. An agent at this place told him there was nothing to be made in the Gold Coast, "nearly all the negroes know how to read and write."

Convention on Forced Labour in 1930 limited the period for public service to a maximum of sixty days in the year and confined the work to able-bodied men.

According to indigenous custom the chief also had the power of drafting labourers for any work which he thought it desirable to undertake. It amounted in practice to the power of conscription, and the imperial Governments have found it a useful means for securing labour for their own purposes. When a supply of workers is required, the district official requisitions a certain number of men from each chief or village headman; chiefs who are progressively minded and co-operate with the Government receive some measure of payment in recognition of their status and their services, while those who cannot meet the demands are fined or imprisoned, and if they prove unfriendly to the administration eventually removed. Thus an investigator who was sent by the French Government to examine the possibilities of cotton growing in the Sudan found that the system of requisitioning labour through the chiefs was "in fact, the ancient Egyptian corvée which existed from the Pharaohs down to the English occupation."[1]

The most effective instrument for rapidly establishing a need of money is undoubtedly a cash tax—it acts alike upon those who have not been accustomed to money, those who do and those who do not want more goods, those who are reluctant to work, and those who dislike employers; in order to pay the tax they must all either sell some produce of their own or work for wages. As a Governor of Kenya pointed out in the early days of that colony, "Taxation is the only possible method of compelling the native to leave his reserve for the purpose of seeking work. Only in this way can the cost of living be increased for the native."[2]

[1] E. Belime, *La Production du Coton en Afrique Française*, quoted by Buell, op. cit., Vol. II, p. 29.

[2] Sir Charles Eliot, quoted Leys, *Kenya*, p. 186.

In all African colonies and protectorates there is now either a poll or hut tax payable in money besides the labour dues for which the natives are liable at certain times. The amount of the tax varies in different places, being 10s. in Northern Rhodesia and 20s. in Southern Rhodesia; $5 in Mozambique and $1.50 in Angola; facilities for earning it, however, also differ, and it is usually the recognition of this by the authorities which accounts for the variation in amount.[1] In some districts the administration now adjusts the annual tax to the conditions affecting wages and prices which are prevailing; in a few it has power to remit the tax altogether if for some unavoidable reason, such as drought or the lack of employment, the natives have no money to pay.[2] It is the first faint beginning of taxation according to capacity to pay, a principle which was not compatible with the purpose for which taxes were first imposed in Africa. In stimulating a labour supply, however, a small tax is usually as effective as a large one, because in order to earn either the native has usually to make a contract for six or nine months' work. And even if he is in a position to grow crops for sale instead, he would not be able to adjust the amount to the value of the tax, but in fact people who willingly grow revenue crops have sufficient sense of monetary values to prefer to spend as small a part as possible in the form of a tax.[3]

A tax is, of course, just as much an involuntary contri-

[1] The incidence of the tax may increase the amount paid by some individuals, e.g. Leys, cit. supra, says that a nominal tax of 12s. requires 28s.–30s. from many able-bodied men because it is calculated on extra huts and dependent relatives.

[2] Belgian Congo, D.O.T. 563, 1933. In 1931 average tax was 41·05 francs per head plus a supplementary tax of 24·16 francs. In 1932 corresponding amounts were 38·67 and 22·78 francs. But still forty thousand natives were arrested for non-payment.

[3] It is significant in this connection that in the British West Indies, where the abolition of slavery left a large class with no alternative to wage-earning, there is neither a poll tax nor a hut tax.

bution as forced labour and can only be obtained on the same principles.[1] At the present time if the failure to pay it can be traced to any defection on the part of the chief he is imprisoned; if the people themselves have omitted to obtain the money they are required to work the tax off at the discretion of the Government; but in the earlier stages of development tax-collecting was accompanied by far more drastic methods of compulsion than these. The mildest method appears to have been the "punitive expedition" of the British, which burnt the huts on which taxes had not been paid, or the kraals of tribes who were in arrears with their poll tax.[2] The French secured the fulfilment of tax obligations by *tournées pacifiques d'impôt*, which aimed at intimidating the natives by physical violence. Fortunately we do not have to undertake here the difficult task of estimating the rights and wrongs of these methods, but as an indication of the feelings which were aroused and the conditions under which the work was carried on, we may note that in 1904 one Chari tribe killed and ate twenty-seven native traders as a protest against the system of taxation.[3] As recently as 1925 the Resident of a district in Cambodia was

[1] The peculiarly autocratic nature of a direct tax in the law of some indigenous people was shown by Mary Kingsley. When the chiefs in Sierra Leone were protesting at the hut tax in 1898, she wrote: "One of the root principles of African law is that the thing you pay anyone a regular fee for is a thing that is not your own—it is a thing belonging to the person to whom you pay the fee . . . that the Government has neither taken this hut from you in war, bought it of you, nor had it given as a gift by you, the owner, vexes you 'too much,' and makes you, if you are any sort of a man, get a gun." Stephen Gwynn, *Life of Mary Kingsley*, p. 174.

[2] Lieut.-Colonel Harding, *Far Bugles*, Chap. XXXII, gives an account of an expedition of this kind against the Barotse.

[3] Buell, op. cit., Vol. II, p. 235. Roberts, *History of French Colonial Policy*, Vol. I, pp. 354-6, mentions that in a tax-collecting raid in the same year, a Congo official imprisoned sixty-eight women in a windowless hut, where forty-seven died, and was promoted. It appears that a high standard was set for natives who might want to undertake reprisals.

killed along with his two assistants in a riot which broke out in a village where he was arresting tax defaulters.[1]

"The reason why the native works when he is told to," said the reply of South Africa to the International Labour Office in 1929, "is because he is afraid something worse will happen to him if he does not." This is probably as good a description of the basis of forced labour as can be given in a few words; it is a system that depends upon penalties for non-performance instead of rewards for performance; and evidence is not lacking that when the labour did not come up to the expectations of the supervisor "something worse" did happen to the native. It would serve no useful purpose to recount here the regime of the *chicote* which was responsible for the "red rubber" of the Congo Free State, the resourceful atrocities that accompanied the recruitment of labour in French Africa, nor the abuses of a "modern slavery" in Portuguese Africa; they were all denounced by contemporary investigators,[2] and they have been regretted —or repudiated—by the highest authorities, yet they continued, and many existed in only a modified form until the economic crisis in 1930 reduced the demand for labour.[3]

[1] At the ensuing trial one native was sentenced to execution, four to hard labour for life, and four to hard labour for fifteen years. Taxes in the province had recently been increased, but even before that the murdered official used to encourage payment by putting the men in gaol. The whole of local opinion was by no means in his favour, and a lively description of the controversy by a contemporary visitor is found in *A Tour in Southern Asia*, Horace Bleachley. *L'Affaire Bardez.*

[2] For instance, A. Vermeesch, *La Question Congolaise*, 1906. E. D. Morel, *Red Rubber*, 1907. G. Toqué, *Les Massacres du Congo*, 1907. F. Challaye, *La Congo Français*, 1909. J. H. Harris, *Down in Darkest Africa*, 1911. W. H. Nevinson, *A Modern Slavery*, 1907. E. A. Ross and others, *Employment of Native Labour in Portuguese Africa*, 1925.

[3] Gide, op. cit., 1925, p. 35, tells of the Yemba case, a native sergeant sent to execute reprisals on a village, who killed thirty men, women, and children by various methods. And not till 1926 were some of the Portuguese abuses curbed by a Convention; while the issue of slavery in Liberia and its relation to labour for the Portuguese islands is still before the League of Nations.

All these coercive practices had one basic principle, the determination to show the native that you were prepared to kill in order to enforce your will; and after a few examples he became tractable. One form of threat which appears to have been both widespread and long-lived was to send a force of native police to a village where they seized the women and children as "hostages," and recruited the men as labourers.[1] Under such a system payment was clearly an irrelevant matter. In 1905 much public attention and indignation was aroused by revelations made at the trial of two officials[2] in the French Congo for the systematic maltreatment, mutilation, and murder of natives under their jurisdiction, and a day-to-day account of the trial was published by de Brazza's assistant, Challaye, who was present. It gives an excellent conspectus of the difficult situation which arose as a result of rapid penetration into a vast country completely unequipped for the purpose of such an administrative system. Toqué was the junior administrator of a Congo province who had not long come out from France, and "il faut faire passer trois mille charges par mois, à têtes d'hommes; c'est une nécessité absolue. Si ces charges ne passent pas, les troupes qui occupent le Tchad manqueront de munitions en face de l'ennemi et mourront de faim. L'administration militaire ayant à son départ laissé à l'administration civile des magasins vides il est rigoureusement impossible de donner aucun salaire aux porteurs. Ces indigènes, qui, même rémunérés, n'acceptent qu'avec dégoût la dure corvée du portage, refusent de s'y soumettre tant qu'ils n'y sont pas contraints. Alors, et bien avant l'arrivée de Toqué, on s'habitue à recruter des

[1] It was often stated that these were ill-treated by the Portuguese police, cf. Olivier, *White Capital and Coloured Labour*, Chap. XV. In French territories, according to the example of Yemba, who burnt a hut with five children in it, on the tax-collecting raid mentioned above, it was apt to be a fatal form of imprisonment.

[2] Toqué and Gaud, vide infra.

porteurs par la force; on les fait enlever dans leur villages par des gardes régionaux; on utilise les 'camps d'otages,' où des femmes et des enfants, entassés en un étroit espace, sont l'objet de toutes les violences et de tous les outrages, meurent de variole et de faim."[1]

From the native point of view this new demand for labour was completely beyond that "legal framework of economic activity" which customarily delimits the range of choice in any society;[2] hence it could only be made operative by pressure from outside, and the view taken by the metropolitan powers as to the urgency of the need dictated the severity of the pressure. According to the evidence available, however, equal severity has been used when the need has been no more urgent than the clearing of land for plantations or the gathering of produce, and the reason for it was the same as in the Toqué incidents, that the authorities initially responsible for instituting the undertaking had not first ascertained the conditions under which their aims would have to take practical shape. Every metropolitan power, it is true, decides the form of development that is to be followed in the territory under its jurisdiction, but after principles and theories have been formulated their execution is effected by local expedients of an empirical character. With few exceptions, no care has been taken to see that specific purposes should not conflict with general principles, and when they did conflict it was the principle which had to give way. It is the colonial official in touch with the natives who must find a means of putting into operation the policies which are arranged by the imperial Government, and in the matter of labour he is constantly confronted with the conflicting duties of protecting native interests and at the same time promoting the interests of the employer. In extensive areas with a sparse official personnel some things are altogether beyond governmental control, and the con-

[1] Challaye, op. cit., p. 141.

[2] Vide supra, Chap. II.

sequent limited effect of legislative provisions has been stated by the Belgian Government with rare candour.[1] The statement points out that Article Two of the law of 1908 for the Congo laid it down that "no person may be compelled to work for or on behalf of individuals or associations," and a Decree of 1922 "strengthens this clause with precautions intended to give the native full freedom of contract." . . . "But," three pages later, "it is evident that a decree of this kind cannot do more than enunciate general principles, which can be applied in many different ways. Its provisions have inevitably left labour conditions in some degree dependent upon the good faith of the employers, each of whom is able to recruit workers on his own account and by his own methods, and subsequently treat them more or less as he pleases."

As we have recognized already, the metropolitan countries all hold backward territories for the definite purpose of bringing them within the orbit of international, or at least imperial, trade, and it is only to be expected that their policies will be directed towards the attainment of this end. Some of them claim that compulsion to labour is not only an efficient but a beneficent instrument for the purpose. It overcomes, say the Portuguese, "L'irrésolution de l'indigène pour le travail, surtout pour le service agricole, que ses traditions considéraient comme déprimantes pour les hommes et seulement propre aux femmes."[2] France has made notable efforts to emphasize the educational aspect

[1] Reply to the Slavery Commission of the League of Nations, A. 25, 1924.

[2] *Code du Travail des Indigènes dans les Colonies Portugaises d'Afrique*, 1931. Portugal has always maintained, in spite of the many eye-witnesses' accounts to the contrary, that the natives under her jurisdiction enjoyed a peculiarly free and happy life. "Not only is our legislation perfect, but its observance is strictly enforced by all the authorities and by special officials," and the allegations of cruelty and oppression were only to be accounted for by "sinister motives" on the part of those who made them. Reply to League Commission on Slavery, A. 18, 1923.

of making the natives undertake work for which they are not naturally inclined, and claims that "the problem of native labour in the colonies is bound up with that of the social education of the native races."[1] Similarly, Belgium claimed that compulsory cultivation was permissible as a measure of education and social welfare.[2]

There has always been a danger that after labourers had been taken away from their homes their employment would degenerate into conditions analogous to slavery. They were separated from their people and their independent resources; the employer could make them work on his own terms, and it usually suited him to pay them as little as possible and keep them as long as possible. One of the chief grounds of protest against labour conditions in the Portuguese colonies was that recruited labour was kept away from home for indefinite periods, and often never returned at all; and another objection was that wages were rarely paid to the labourers themselves, but to the chief who sent them or the officials who procured them.[3] The metropolitan powers have agreed in recent years to try to prevent these slave conditions from arising by providing for the payment in cash of all labourers, and limiting the period for which natives may be kept away from home; and the International Draft Convention on Forced Labour prohibits the use of such labour by private employers. A delicate point in connection with the last provision arises when Government officials are allowed to hold and work concessions for their private profit, as they do in Portuguese Africa, and use their administrative position to obtain labour.[4]

When all available labour is not wanted for plantations, another form of pressure to increase production is found in COMPULSORY CULTIVATION. In general aspect this recalls

[1] I.L.O., cit. supra. [2] Ibid.

[3] Ross Report, cit. supra. and Cmd. 6322, 1909.

[4] Ibid. and Olivier, cit. supra.

the forced deliveries and culture system by which the Dutch increased the production of Java and their own revenue from the colony in earlier times, but some modern changes have been made in the method of payment. "Comment developper l'agriculture sans cultivateurs actifs?" was the difficulty that had to be overcome in the Belgian Congo, says a Minister of Colonies,[1] and in 1917 the Government introduced the system of *cultures obligatoires.* Natives in certain districts were ordered to plant a prescribed quantity of food crops which were bought directly by the Government and either exported or sent to the industrial area of the Katanga. "Ce fut grâce a ce système de cultures obligatoires," says M. Leplae, "imposées, faut-il-dire, avec une très grande modération, que la Colonie produit bientôt de fortes quantités de riz dans la Province Orientale et commença la culture du coton dans la Maniema et les Ueles. La méthode reçut bientôt des applications dans toutes les régions de la Colonie."[2] Both France and Belgium have emphasized the educational nature of this method of production in their replies to the International Labour Office.[3]

In 1918 a Native Plantations Ordinance was introduced into Papua in order to increase cultivation and improve native agriculture. "In fact," says Sir Hubert Murray, "the system works out very much as follows. The Government resumes an area of land near a village and calls it a Native Plantation. The natives, or a certain number of them, work out their tax by clearing, planting, etc., while the Government superintends and supplies seed and tools. The crop is divided between the Government and the villagers, and the proceeds of the Government's share are paid into the same account as the tax, and consequently can only be

[1] Ed. Leplae, *Méthode Suivie pour le Développement de l'Agriculture du Congo Belge*, Congo, October 1930.

[2] Ibid., p. 386.

[3] I.L.O. Report, cit. supra.

expended for the direct benefit of the natives.[1] In the Mandated Territory of New Guinea it is also the aim of the administration to increase the natives' production by compelling them to plant larger areas.[2]

If imposed industry of this sort develops an aptitude for the new economic system which could not otherwise be acquired; if it gives an initial impulse in the direction of capitalistic production and then leaves the natives willing to continue on their own initiative, it is a valuable method of development; and by leaving the natives a share in the proceeds of their crop it can escape the censure now levelled at the more extortionate forms of coercion. The one condition required for this successful outcome is that the natives should distinguish between education and slavery. If the effect of compulsion at the beginning is that they never show any initiative on their own behalf it will probably do nothing except add resentment to apathy.[3]

Because it has so frequently been associated with violence, abuse, and exploitation in its crudest meaning, forced labour has earned a separate category in the history of tropical development. CONTRACT LABOUR represents an attempt to protect the native from these abuses by guaranteeing his working conditions and remuneration before he is recruited, and at the same time to provide the employer with a

[1] Op. cit. supra, p. 272.

[2] *Report on the Territory*, 1930–31. In the annual records of cases heard by the Courts of Native Authority, convictions are found for "Failing to plant sufficient crops for his own requirements" and for "Disobeying lawful order to tend crops."

[3] As early as 1902 the Germans made a regulation in Samoa that each head of a family was to plant fifty coconuts yearly, and this led to the growing of over a million new trees—but by 1913 the native production of copra showed no increase over what it had been before the trees were planted. The Royal Commission on East Africa recognized that there was "great danger in Africa lest a man once compelled should take up the attitude that he will not work unless he is compelled." Cmd. 2387, 1925.

reliable labour force for a definite period. Soon after the formal abolition of slavery by Great Britain recruiters of labour began to use a form of contract which was enough to satisfy the Government that involuntary servitude was not being imposed, but which was, in fact, nothing but a trap for labourers ignorant of the obligations they assumed; in practice this "indenture system," used chiefly to secure the migration of Indian and Kanaka labourers to other areas, was accompanied by the same conditions that had been characteristic of slavery.[1] At the present time, however, the labour contract is supposed to be freely entered into by both the parties, whose rights it defines and protects; and in most territories it must be signed in the presence of a Government official whose duty it is to see that the natives understand the terms.[2] The agreement stipulates the period the native shall work, the pay he shall receive, and the food, clothing, and housing which the employer must provide. From the circumstances in which he lives it is virtually impossible to secure redress by civil process from a native for breach of contract, and therefore the law in most territories provides penal sanctions for such a breach. At the same time penalties are prescribed for "crimping" or "decoying" because, as the Royal Commission on Labour in India recognized, it is important to ensure that the labourer will work on the plantation which has paid the cost of recruiting and transporting him.[3]

[1] *Report on Emigration from India to the Crown Colonies and Protectorates*, Cd. 5192, 1909, gives exhaustive information on the Indian emigration. *Report on Indentured Labour in Fiji*, by Andrews and Pearson, gives additional information for this colony.

[2] Orde Browne, op. cit., Chap. XI, "The Contract," and Chap. XII, "The Value of the Contract," discusses the difference between old and new methods of recruitment, and the importance of making the native feel that he is treated fairly. Similarly, De Kat Angelino, op. cit., Chap. VII, Vol. II, claims that the contract in the Dutch Indies gives security to worker as well as employer.

[3] Cmd. 3883, 1931, Chap. XIX.

The method of recruitment is clearly an important factor in the functioning of this system. Indeed, if it is a system intended to eliminate all compulsion from the distribution of native labour, one may even wonder why such strict organization is necessary. The day of the reckless and irresponsible recruiter who merely sought hasty profits from a temporary venture is over.[1] Recruiting is now conducted either by an official bureau or by agents licensed by the Governments, and agreements are obtained from the natives by methods that range from merely spreading information about the openings for employment to exercising official persuasion to work which they cannot distinguish from a command. Recruiting by force may not be permitted, but as the Governor-General of the Belgian Congo wrote in 1925, "Is this to say that the territorial authority should abstain from using all the moral persuasion which he possesses to furnish labourers to the mines? Assuredly not."[2] And according to the East Africa Commission, "The native must be taught that unless he is prepared to do a reasonable amount of work on his own account it is his duty to go out to work either for Government or private employers."[3]

The final test by which recruiting must be judged is whether it stimulates a regular supply of willing labour, or whether it relies on an element of coercion which secures involuntary, and therefore low-grade, workers; and in this respect it is only a particular case of the general problem of forced labour. In so far as initial pressure or persuasion supplies the natives with lasting motives for earning wages it fulfils its aim of promoting a regular supply of labour;

[1] Orde Browne, idem.

[2] Quoted by Buell, op. cit., Vol. II, p. 543.

[3] Cmd. 2387, 1925. In connection with the exercise of persuasion it is interesting to note that resentment at the contracting of labourers in Tonkin led to an anti-recruiting campaign in 1928, in the course of which the Director of the Employment Office was murdered. I.L.R., October 1931.

but it is an inherent danger of all measures of compulsion that conditions and occupations which are in the first place associated with coercion come to be permanently regarded with aversion, and by paying too little attention to possibilities of inducement modern employment can perpetuate precisely those characteristics which were undesirable and inefficient in slave labour.[1]

The problem of establishing a capitalistic system in backward territories is that of grafting a structure which arose in one place in consequence of a certain set of conditions on to a completely different set of conditions in another place, and the degree of success which the enterprise will enjoy depends upon the ratio of efficiency with which the old factors of production, land and labour, are combined with the new factor, capital. The cost and the supply of labour are two important interrelated problems. In the first place a sufficient supply of voluntary labour cannot be induced to work for its productivity rate of wages—or possibly for the lower rate which employers without competition are offering—and so political measures are invoked to compel a supply. But the use of compulsion is likely to reduce both the efficiency of the labour in the short run and the total supply in the long run. The necessity for constant supervision of unskilled native labour is in any case a large addition to its cost, and the more unwilling the workers are the less effort does their labour time represent.[2] Thus the amount of productivity can be diminished although the supply of numbers is maintained.

[1] Orde Browne, cit. supra, p. 30. Cairnes, in the *Slave Power*, Chap. II, "The Economic Basis of Slavery," discusses the effect of lack of incentive on the productivity of the slave.

[2] Orde Browne, cit. supra, discusses this in Africa. The compulsory labour system in Tanganyika before the War resulted in a short week, a short day, a small task, which proved an expensive and unsatisfactory way of using labour. *Report upon Labour in Tanganyika Territory*, 1925, Colonial No. 19.

Munro, *The Central American Republics*, p. 64, contrasts the low pro-

In the long run even the numbers will not be kept up by wholly arbitrary measures, and the use of land and capital will be curtailed by the scarcity of labour, which means that the new economic system defeats its ends by its methods. Whenever foreign labour requirements have been drastically enforced with total disregard of native views and wishes in the matter, decay of the local population has been rapid. This was shown by the early rubber-gathering regime in the Congo Free State;[1] the effects of it can still be observed in some parts of French Equatorial Africa,[2] while in other French territories migration has been prohibited in an effort to prevent the evasion of military and labour services;[3] and after protests from many sources had gone unheeded, it was the exhaustion of supplies that put an end to the transportation of Pacific islanders to plantations in Queensland.[4] With this effect of arbitrary innovations upon population movements it is significant to compare the consequences of the culture system imposed by the Dutch upon the

ductivity of the Guatemalan *peon* with that of the free Costa Rican and Salvadorean peasant, whose wages are 400–800 per cent higher than those in Guatemala.

It is interesting to compare with this experience of indigenous labour the expense and ultimate failure of the attempt to use convicts from France as labour in New Caledonia. Roberts, *Population Problems of the Pacific*, p. 282.

[1] Buell, op. cit., Vol. II, Chap. LXXXVIII, says that the dual problem which confronted Leopold's successors was a disintegrating population and a pressing need for labour.

[2] Gide, op. cit., p. 78, says that the penalties for enforcing rubber collection were making inhabitants flee from the villages. And Challaye, op. cit., says that de Brazza found that previously inhabited tracts in the Congo had been abandoned.

[3] Still, however, successive census enumerations in the British West African areas show an increased number of "Foreign Africans."

[4] Sir John Harris, *A Century of Emancipation*, p. 135: "In 1898 the Aborigines Protection Society was able to report that 'the difficulties of obtaining a supply of recruits from islands already deprived of so many of their inhabitants . . . rendered this form of slavery so costly and inconvenient that it is ceasing to be profitable.' "

indigenous economy of Java. The system introduced by Van der Bosch in 1830 rested upon an indigenous basis meant for entirely different situations and methods, and "the heavy systematic organization soon sagged right through the basis of magical mysticism, partially disorganizing village society and its agrarian system. Land property lost much of its attraction in certain districts, because all the burdens imposed from above through the channel of the village administration pressed exclusively upon the landowners according to the ancient Adat rule that social rights and social duties form one inseparable whole."[1] The duties having been increased, people were unwilling to accept the rights, and it became impossible to find a holder for a comparatively large area, so that the land had to be parcelled out in as many small portions as possible.

The statement is frequently found in recent writings on the subject of native labour, especially in Africa, that an employer can obtain voluntary labour without difficulty if it is known that he treats his labourers well—as the East African Commission put it, "the problem of African labour still remains very largely personal." This is undoubtedly true; the African is no less discriminating in his choice of working conditions when he has the opportunity of choosing than other workers would be, and he would naturally not choose a plantation where he was starved and menaced if he knew one where he would be well fed and reasonably instructed. But why is he choosing between plantations at all? It is necessary to connect with this employment situation the system of taxation and other wage-earning "stimuli" to which the natives have been subjected, a fundamental factor which the commentators on the relative attractions of employment usually ignore. Native labour has been made a personal problem by its political background; the labourers

[1] De Kat Angelino, Vol. II, p. 436.

do not consider the attractions of different occupations until they have felt the need to do the work. And so successfully has this need been established that the decrease in employment which followed the fall of prices in 1930 has led to difficulty, and even distress, in some places.[1]

[1] *Tanganyika, Report of Native Administration*, 1932. "There have been thousands of natives out of employment . . . who are unable to pay their tax and who do not get one square meal a day."

N. Leys, *A Last Chance in Kenya*, 1931: "In the early autumn of 1931 the labour market is glutted by gangs of men wandering over the country, offering themselves at 8s. a thirty-day period, and finding none to hire them."

Belgian Congo, Labour Y.C.C.D., 1932, p. 57. "Le nombre des travailleurs actuellement disponibles est très élevé et la préoccupation du moment est plutôt de trouver de la besogne pour les licenciés."

CHAPTER V

MONETARY INCENTIVES AND THE STANDARD OF LIVING

THE policies for obtaining labour which we have examined so far all belong to the method of imposing new obligations on the native; when they introduce the use of money it is as a coercive measure. None of them encourages a voluntary expansion of the wants that an increased labour effort would supply. What we must now consider is the creation of new wants which would provide the natives with a motive for earning money to spend on ends of their own choice. The first thing to be noticed is that this has never been the immediate object of governmental policy. It has happened that in the course of his experience with forced labour the native has often acquired a taste for the things that money can buy, and many tribesmen now work outside their reserves for the sake of obtaining goods no less than taxes. But although the basis of modern tropical colonization has been that *die Flagge folgt dem Handel*, no metropolitan power has relied on the spread of commodity wants to stimulate a native labour supply.[1] In fact it is not an extreme statement that early tropical development proceeded on the principle that an atrocity was better than an expense. The atrocities have been repudiated or regretted, but at the same time it has been claimed that the expense of inducements would be useless. And while this contention has sometimes been made to justify particular instances of

[1] This statement might not appear universally applicable from the point of view as expressed by Lord Lugard, for example, that because Government has never supported compulsory labour for private purposes in British West Africa "employers must, therefore, make the conditions of service sufficiently attractive to secure the labourers they need." But direct taxes were imposed in British West Africa, and labour for Government purposes was recruited through the chiefs.

cheaper extortion, it has also gained such widespread credence in places disinterested and even benevolent that it deserves careful consideration.

The theory that the native will necessarily fail to respond to monetary inducement is found in two parts. The first claims that he is inherently lacking in the capacity to appreciate the purchasing power of money and must therefore be converted to the desirable habit of wage-earning by forcible means. When this has been done, the second part of the theory appears and declares that he is constitutionally incapable of enjoying more than his customary exiguous standard of living, and cannot therefore be paid higher wages because he would work less. Mr. Joseph Chamberlain, who originated the idea of treating the colonies as "Imperial estates," had to consider the relation of the natives to his purpose, and his aim was to "induce them to adopt the ordinary methods of earning a livelihood by the sweat of their brow"—although he doubted if it could be done by preaching.[1] The same conception of the high principle, an ethical obligation incumbent on the deserving, that is embodied in a regular wage-earning routine has continued to pervade the imperial attitude to natives' labour; they must be taught that it is "their duty to work at industrial employment."[2] A similar idea underlies the defence by Latin countries of compulsory labour as a means of education.[3] It envisages the transplanting of proletarian habits to places where natural conditions had not created a proletariate. For a long time Europe had been building a doctrine of salvation on the necessity of working hard for a living, and by the nineteenth century Europeans

[1] Knowles, op. cit., p. 278. [2] Cmd. 2387, 1925. Cit. supra.

[3] Albert Sarraut, *La Mise en Valeur des Colonies Françaises*, puts it impeccably: "Instruire l'indigène est assurément notre devoir; c'est une obligation morale impérieuse que nous créent les responsabilités de la souveraineté vis-à-vis des populations indigènes dont nous avons assumé la tutelle."

could think of no better fate for Africans. But it was a fate that had to be compelled.

In the actual circumstances, without deductive theories of society and progress, it could not have been intelligently anticipated that the tropical native would regard the profitable disposition of his energies as a Calvinistic abnegation of more self-indulgent pursuits; the required stimulus was exactly the opposite—that his epicurean desires should find enlarged opportunities of gratification. It is claimed that indentured labour is necessary in Papua because "free labour postulated certain qualities which the Papuan lacks, e.g. determination and perseverance."[1] But these qualities are only of significance in so far as they are directed to a definite purpose, and the Papuans, as well as other people, must have had them in a sufficient degree to serve the ends of their indigenous economy; their defection under European standards was due to the different ends which these imposed. The essential points which the best and the worst policies of tropical development ignored was that of providing the natives with an attractive purpose for altering their economy. It was not more virtuous habits that they wanted, but more pleasing alternatives to those thay had.[2] Probably Europe could not provide any better for the established wants of the natives than they could provide themselves, and it was to these wants—food and tobacco—that Mary Kingsley and others referred when they said that the natives were in need of nothing. But there were other wants—bicycles, gramophones, and cinemas—which had hitherto been outside the scope of their economy, but which they had no aversion to acquiring.[3]

This introduction of new wants is closely connected with

[1] Murray, op. cit., p. 260.

[2] "Quant au travail forcé, lorsque indigène trouve son profit dans le travail qu'on lui demande, toute contrainte devient inutile." Duke of Brabant, speech in Senate, July 25, 1933.

[3] Orde Browne, *Vanishing Tribes of Kenya*, p. 267, and M. Mead, *Coming of Age in Samoa*, Appendix 3, discuss the new goods adopted by natives.

the second part of the money theory—that higher wages are an incentive to less instead of more work. "The negro is so constituted," says one large employer, "that if he can earn by one day's labour sufficient to satisfy his needs for a whole week he will prefer to work one day and live in idleness through the other six,"[1] and a similar opinion has dominated most labour organization in the tropics. Obviously it rests on the assumption that the native's needs are at any time unalterably fixed, that his demand schedule is perfectly inelastic, and his tastes totally insusceptible to new attractions. Is it tenable that such an attitude is absolute, or should it be regarded as depending upon relative conditions of supply? It has happened that on some occasions when agents increased the rate they paid natives for rubber or ivory in order to obtain larger supplies when prices were rising, the amount offered for sale by the natives declined, and this was an indication that under existing conditions their demand for money was inelastic. But such a rigid delimitation of wants has not been known to continue in the face of increasing offers of new goods, and the native's monetary calculus is directly correlated with the changing structure of his wants.[2]

The adaptation of productive effort to an exchange economy is essentially a matter of substituting ends which an increasing supply of money will serve for those that have customarily been satisfied by a fixed amount of labour. The interest of the native in making the change is, therefore, retarded by anything that either hinders his acquaintance with possible new ends or makes the means of attaining

[1] Sir Robert Williams, *Milestones from Cape Town to Cairo,* United Empire, January 1933.

[2] "When a native takes produce to market it is from no abstract desire for possession of money; he has in his mind a definite object on which the proceeds are to be spent. If he has no such object he will let the surplus product of his garden or net decay, rather than undergo the trouble of taking it to market." *Fijian Commission on Depopulation,* 1893. Cited Roberts, *Problems of the Pacific,* p. 224.

them unduly onerous. Thus the chief factors which tend to resist innovations and rigidify traditional demand schedules are antagonizing early contacts, such as ill-treatment or oppression, with the new methods of production, and a Government policy of regimenting indigenous economy by a system of segregated reserves and restraints on native enterprise outside.[1] And apart from these positive discouragements, it does not appear that the incentive of high wages has actually been tried as often as its failure to stimulate productive effort has been lamented. The Royal Commission on Labour in India, for instance, did not believe that there was substance in the employers' claims that labourers would not respond to wage inducements,[2] and it has been pointed out in the case of South Africa that with the native standard of living rising it is an invalid argument that with higher wages he will work less; "the main effect of higher wages is that the native buys more goods."[3] Moreover, it has sometimes been apparent that wage labour was scarce because the natives could earn more by independent production, and therefore preferred this form of occupation, and such a choice shows a direct response to a higher level of remuneration.[4]

[1] P. G. Mockerie, *An African Speaks for His People*, p. 63, says, in denial of the claim that education of the natives will check the labour supply, "when a person is well educated he feels ashamed to be hungry and naked; his requirements are many; he wants good food, clothes and a house. Now where is he going to get these things in order to satisfy his requirements? He will be compelled to work by economic circumstances."

The obverse view of the same point is stated by W. H. Hutt, "Economic Aspects of the Poor White Commission," *South African Journal of Economics*, September 1933, in rejecting the assumption that the low standard of living of the native has a depressing effect on wages, "the more content a native population is with its traditional standards, the less will it compete for outside employment."

[2] Cmd. 3883, 1931, cit. supra.

[3] *Round Table*, June 1928, "The African Labour Problem."

[4] The difficulty that arises from disproportionate earnings is clearly shown in *Rap. An. du Congo Belge*, 1924. "Industrial and commercial

Not the rashest proponent of the theory of native insensibility to monetary inducement has said that given the opportunity the natives cannot spend money. What is claimed is that they will not earn it. Now if they are unwilling to work for the wages offered, it must be because the purchasing power these represent is less than the value of the same labour spent on direct production, or too low to be worth the required sacrifice of time and effort. Then the relevant question is, What determines the rate of wages? It cannot rise above the productivity value of the labour, and in a free economy with competition between employers the worker will get his productivity wage. But another aspect from which the age level is often regarded is that of the standard of living of labour, that is, of the workers' requirements for satisfying their habitual wants, and European employers have usually chosen their conception of the native standard of living as indicative of an appropriate rate of wages. Unfortunately, however, they do not always appreciate the less tangible elements of the standard which are of importance to the native. Because he lives in the European view on a mere subsistence level, it does not mean that he likes equally well to subsist in the supervised ranks of a labour camp and the companionable freedom of his village. He may easily find the European alternative too high a price for mere subsistence, and if he does, a free labour market must offer him something more in order to induce him to pay the price. That is to say, unless the native is not to be permitted a free economy, the scale of preferences which constitutes his standard of living must be of his own determination.

In a free economy, the cost of the inducement the employer

enterprises encounter a thousand difficulties in securing necessary labour which is due to the disproportion existing between the price of a day's work and the rate at which wild produce gathered in the forest may be sold. In a few days the native can earn the monthly wage of a labourer in European employment." Quoted by Buell, Vol. II, p. 544.

can offer to workers depends directly upon the productivity value of their labour; and when in the transition stages of a self-sufficient economy the standard of living does not have to adjust itself to ruling market values, because the natives have an alternative means of living available, there may easily be a gap between what their labour is worth to an employer and the price they set upon their time and effort. As we have seen, the method usually adopted for overcoming this difficulty has been arbitrary coercion of the native standard of living; but from another point of view the problem was one of equating the productivity rate of the labourers with their demand schedules for money, and this outlook would indicate an employment policy which aims at raising the value of the native's exchange production to the level which would attract him to the work. This could be done by providing additional capital and organizing output on a basis which endowed labour with a higher earning capacity. And if conditions are such that the substitution of capital for labour is impracticable, or managerial ability is too scarce for efficient use to be made of the factors that are available, and hence, in the view of the Governments and concessionaires concerned, there is no alternative to making labour cheap by coercion, then the native who withholds his labour is acting from the same motive as the employer who withholds his capital—that it would be unprofitable to use it at the prevailing price. In fact, what is condemned as laziness or dislike of work on the part of the native has often been in essentials a reluctance to expend a large amount of effort upon inefficient and poorly remunerated forms of labour.[1]

[1] When working on his own behalf the native shows a keen appreciation of the significance of price variations, and is willing to expend extra effort in obtaining money he wants. For instance, Dudgeon, op. cit., p. 56, says of the early days of cacao farming in the Gold Coast, "the report that at another town, often distant by many days' journey, a higher price is being paid than that obtained in a market close at

A policy of increasing the productivity value of native labour rests, of course, on the assumption that higher wages will be an incentive to voluntary effort. If you believe that a higher rate of pay would be "a direct encouragement to idleness,"[1] which amounts to saying that the native's demand for leisure alone is elastic and all the other elements in his standard of living are fixed beyond the lure of avarice or vanity, then the longer you want him to work the less you must pay him.[2] But in practice this is exactly the situation which gives rise to labour difficulties. There are no complaints of the members of any race refusing to take well-paid positions, or those of a less onerous kind. The Malay, for instance, who will not work on a plantation willingly

hand, will frequently induce a native to convey his head-loads to the distant market, regardless of the fact that the extra shilling or so he may receive does not appear to be sufficient compensation for the additional time and effort." Of course, it must seem sufficient to the native or he would not make the effort. That he does so shows his readiness to respond to monetary inducement when it serves his interests.

[1] Sir Robert Williams, loc. cit. supra.

[2] It is interesting to compare with this modern view of primitive labour the strikingly similar attitude to contemporary labour in *American Economic Thought in the Seventeenth Century*, E. A. J. Johnson, Chap. II, "Wages and Usury." Land was free, labour was scarce, and the colonial rulers grudged high wages. They argued that in consequence of high wages, "(i.) Many spent much time idly, etc., because they could get as much in four days as would keep them a week. (ii.) They spent much in tobacco and strong waters, etc., which was a great waste to the Commonwealth."

"This statement," says the author, "is merely a sample of the great number of similar complaints in the colonial records. The persistent belief that high wages were socially and morally dangerous continued through the seventeenth century and far into the eighteenth, until it was answered with extraordinary ability by Adam Smith." Nevertheless, he continues, page 211: "It is true, of course, that backward people, with inflexible standards of living, may be tempted to idleness by high wages, but the general mercantile fallacy had no such anthropological basis." Surely anthropology cannot be said to be the basis of the labour fallacy of to-day. And had the science existed then, it would no doubt have found much that was backward in Europe of the seventeenth century, where standards of living had been inflexible for a long time.

becomes a policeman or a chauffeur; the best Philippino labour left agricultural for artisan employment; neither in East nor West Africa is there difficulty in obtaining natives for the more skilled occupations; and in all places where the higher grades of employment are open to them it is lack of training and not unwillingness that restricts their numbers. In parts of Central America where landowners had long complained that voluntary labour was insufficient or unobtainable, a foreign company has found it possible to work large banana plantations with free labour paid a higher rate than that prevailing for other occupations in the neighbourhood, and both well managed and fully equipped with capital facilities.[1]

For evidence of labour that is neither satisfactory nor enterprising we must turn to other conditions. "Hard work in an unhealthful climate, low wages, and a pernicious system of bondage dependent upon keeping him perpetually in debt, make of the *cholo* a listless and backward specimen of humanity. Plantations can secure relatively efficient labour only by constant and expensive supervision."[2] And, as we saw before, these results are to be expected when neither the conditions nor the reward of labour take the form of an inducement to work. If they are left to the habitual conditions of their indigenous economy, any people will find sufficient inducement to exertion in the necessity of obtaining subsistence, but the stimulus to making a

[1] C. F. Jones, *South America*, describes the system in Colombia, p. 584. The same method has succeeded in Guatemala and Honduras. D. G. Munro, *The Five Republics of Central America*, p. 134.

[2] Jones, cit. supra, referring to Ecuador, p. 518. Comparable with this statement is the description of the peonage system introduced in Guatemala for the coffee plantations. "Under the present system, the under-fed and ill-treated Indians are unwilling and inefficient workers, and their services involve a great deal of extra expense to the employer in the form of sums to be paid to local officials in return for aid in contracting them." Yet in the same country Indians are growing market crops on their own account. Munro, cit. supra, p. 64.

change in those conditions depends upon the improvement in the standard of living it offers.[1] It is a contradictory policy, therefore, to try and introduce new methods of employment without at the same time providing for some added attractions to the standard of living. Just as new wants are additional to old, so must new occupations be more remunerative than old. It is the endeavour to effect a substitution of new things and new methods without offering any additional benefits which has been largely responsible for the theory that the native is proof against "economic inducement."

Another source of misunderstanding is that the advantages which a backward people is likely to desire from a change of ends will most probably not be such as the European attitude to social progress would indicate. A native's rising standard of living does not show the same order of wants as is familiar in Europe; he spends more on pleasure and less on status, and wants a bicycle or a gramophone before he considers better housing.[2] The consequence of this incidence of desire is that he appears in foreign eyes to be a person of extravagance and thriftlessness, who enjoys luxuries and ignores respectability. But actually this scale of preferences shows a quite reasonable principle of cultural osmosis. It is in the primary categories of wants, in the mere subsistence stratum, that habit and custom is most conservative

[1] It is significant that the *Report on Labour in Tanganyika Territory* for 1933 comments on the "apparent paradox" that the depression should result in a "shortage of labour, especially in the completely unskilled type which draws the lowest scale of wages." Clearly it is this level of remuneration which offers least advantages to the native and first becomes less attractive than independence when wages are reduced.

[2] Sir Robert Williams, cit. supra, speaks of the wage basis of the white standard of living as being beyond the black worker's "requirements or his ability to enjoy," but these are two different things. The native need not have the same "requirements" in order to enjoy the same wage. It is easily conceivable that he will get more enjoyment from spending it on other things than the white worker finds necessary.

and hence demand is least elastic.[1] In the higher classes of consumption goods the limitation is not so rigid, and innovations depend to a greater extent on the satisfaction they give. Thus, however tenaciously rice-eating, wheat-eating, and banana-eating peoples cling to their respective diets, they will show some disposition to appreciate the same textiles and utensils; and when the level of moving pictures and motor-cars is reached, neither race, religion, nor previous custom is a factor in regulating demand; it is financial competence alone that determines the consumption of Bantu, Indian, and European. And the native whose family grows his food, and whose clothing requirements are not exacting, is in the fortunate position of being able to spend his earnings on pleasures undulled by a sense of necessity—except so far as the Government dims the prospect with taxes or the chief with levies. Yet the fact that he does spend his money in this way has given rise to criticism, anxiety, and sometimes commiseration on the part of foreign observers, who regard it as a waste of hard-earned wages and a failure to distinguish what is worthless from what might be worth while. But can anything accurately be said to be worthless if somebody is willing to pay a price for it? And who knows the value of money better than the person who has worked for it? There may be no useful service that an umbrella can perform for a naked inhabitant of the jungle,[2] but need the charm of possessing it be less on that

[1] J. T. McCurdy, *Mind and Money*, p. 13, says that the psychologist "finds that there is a general law to the effect that the more restricted the diet (in animals or men) the harder it is to induce the subject to eat anything new."

[2] A. Gide, op. cit., p. 530, recounts with satisfaction how, having paid off the porters he had for his Congo journey at Douala, he was just in time to prevent them buying umbrellas at 35 francs each. Similarly, L. P. Mair, *An African People in the Twentieth Century*, p. 7, says, "the native has no idea of money values and will sacrifice a month's wage for a worthless object." The point with which we are concerned here is that he must want the object. It is the wanting which stimulates

account? There is no measure of values known to economic science except the individual's estimate of his own satisfaction, and if any other standards of judgment are applicable to the charms of possession they seldom appear to be operative. Civilized people buy all the useless things they can afford, and the process gives some of the things a very high value. If a liking for leisure is a culpable characteristic of tropical people, the remedy is that the more things they want, however useless, the better citizens they will be.[1]

In conclusion, we must note that where a process of labour inducement such as we have been discussing becomes effective, it makes a change in the native standard of living which is permanent. Henceforth that standard will include wants that can only be satisfied by the possession of purchasing power. When any community of natives have become accustomed to money economy and dependent upon exchange production, it cannot, therefore, be fairly said that the failure of markets or wage employment does not give rise to difficulty because the workers can return to their own land.[2] It is true that as long as they can grow food they need not starve, but they are no further removed from "destitution" than are the unemployed workers in other countries who cultivate an allotment as the only alternative

working. The particular wants which may or may not be desirable from the governmental point of view are, of course, an entirely different matter. But it was pointed out above that an imposed scale of values may fail to arouse enthusiasm in the native.

[1] As an example of how the European attitude has impressed this standard of merit upon other races, we have the appeal of Booker Washington to the American Negroes to "want more wants" in order to improve their status.

[2] That no difficulty is created by such a situation is evidently accepted by Orde Browne, *The African Labourer*, p. 112. And the *Report on Labour in Tanganyika Territory*, cit. supra, remarks that "this independence of labour has been a great advantage to the industries of the country during the hard struggles of the past year or two." This is, no doubt, true, but one would expect a Department of Native Affairs to consider whether it is a form of independence that the native likes to exercise.

to the money income which is what they really want. In so far as the native becomes a money-earner he is assimilated to capitalist economy, and capitalism inculcates pecuniary motives of production and dissolves the old tribal limitations. Hence the native acquires new economic concepts, and once the elasticity of demand for consumption goods has raised his standard of living, the process cannot be reversed without causing a feeling of hardship.[1]

[1] Some examples of such hardship in different places were given at the end of the previous chapter. Further, as evidence of the difficulty of dispensing with accustomed exchange goods we may take the situation in the Netherlands Indies, *Yearbook of Agricultural Co-operation*, 1934, p. 217. "The native people cannot even make the modest prices for their products that cover their low expenses. Necessity squeezes out of them whatever of gold value they possess: forty million guilders' worth of gold jewellery have been melted and exported."

CHAPTER VI

CONTEMPORARY METHODS OF PRODUCTION

I. THE PLANTATION SYSTEM

THE form in which foreign enterprise is conducted in the tropics is either that of *concessions* for a stated period over areas of natural products, or of freehold or leasehold grants for the purpose of *plantation* cultivation. Since the seventeenth century the plantation has been the dominant method of European agricultural development in tropical regions. In the earlier periods there was little mechanical equipment, even less scientific cultivation, and labour represented a capital investment in the form of slaves, while land was usually a free gift. The present situation is exactly opposite in almost every respect. Land is obtained by rent or purchase—although the price is in some places low—labour is paid money wages, methods of increasing the fertility of the soil have greatly improved, and in every industry capital is extensively employed. The form of cultivation that may legitimately be called plantation production now represents a permanent investment and a long-term interest in a defined area of land.

Concessions have in a few instances developed into plantations, but more often, and especially when the area conceded was very large, they have not developed at all. The concessions regime which followed the demarcation of European spheres in Africa in the nineteenth century was in essentials a recrudescence of the simple system of wealth extraction which the Spaniards had practised in America. It was a method of exploitation which the French called *cueillette* and the Germans *raubbau,* and which aimed at securing rubber, ivory, and anything else that was marketable, by compelling the natives to collect it and without making any positive contribution to cultivation. Many of these original concessions have lapsed, or been forfeited through the failure of the grantees to undertake the amount of cultivation which would have given them a freehold title, and the area of most of the remainder has been reduced to the manageable dimensions of a plantation.[1] In the republics of tropical South America and in Central America, however, many of the vast estates granted to the Conquistadores are still owned by their descendants, and for the most part are only partially cultivated.[2] But although these may appear to be deficient in capital and lacking in enterprise when compared with European plantations in other countries, since they do represent a permanent interest of the landowner and a settled form of cultivation they are a part of the plantation system. Under the influence of varying local and labour conditions and different cultivation requirements this system shows many modifications, and while it is distinguished on the one hand from a *cueillette* regime by its permanent investment aspect, it is also distinguished at

[1] The Treaty, which made the *Congo Free State* into a colony of Belgium, recognized seven foreign concessions amounting to over 52 million hectares and five of these had been considerably reduced from their original limits. The largest was 46,788,000 hectares of the Comité Special du Katanga, an area regarded as suitable for European settlement, which has large mineral deposits. Buell, op. cit., Vol. II, p. 537. In 1930 there was little more than 100,000 hectares of plantation cultivation. In 1910 the concessions in *French Equatorial Africa* were revised and "instead of thirty-eight companies having exclusive rights over 874,140 sq. kilometres, as in 1889, hereafter there were a few companies in the coastal and middle regions and one combine in the far interior. By giving increased rights over 3,800 sq. kilometres, the Government secured the reversion of 300,000 sq. kilometres—an area that doubled by 1923." Roberts, *French Colonial Policy*, p. 359. The early estimates of population in this region were 10–12 million; it is now counted at three and a half million—insufficient, even if it had been willing, for the thorough cultivation of such vast areas. In 1929 the Portuguese Government resumed the 73,500 sq. miles of the Niassa Co.

[2] C. F. Jones, op. cit., pp. 188, 257, 520, 518. D. G. Munro, op. cit., p. 3.

the other end of the scale from peasant proprietorship in being essentially a large-scale method of production, involving the centralized management of extensive lands and a large labour force. A survey of plantation organization in various parts of the tropics at the present time shows several forms.

1. Freehold or long leasehold land, and casual local labour. This form of organization prevails in the British and French West Indies, Cuba, and Porto Rico, under the fruit companies in the Caribbean republics, on a million acres held by foreign planters on seventy-five years' lease from the Government of Java, and is usual wherever native owners work plantations, e.g. in Sumatra, Malaya, Ceylon, the Gold Coast, and Zanzibar, although Europeans in the same regions use contract labour.

2. Freehold or leasehold land and contract indigenous labour. This situation is associated chiefly with Africa, and is the leading form of organization in African territories of every nationality.

3. Freehold or leasehold land and contract immigrant labour. When local labour was not available, and the Government was not opposed to Indian and Chinese immigration, this has been the chief means of plantation development. It was introduced into Mauritius, Fiji, Trinidad, British Guiana, and Jamaica by a system of indenture, which was subsequently abolished, and prevails now in the form of civil contract in Ceylon, Malaya, Assam, and Hawaii. In all these territories a large number of the labourers remain voluntarily after the expiration of their first contracts, and become comparable to casual labour.

4. In a few places indentured labour is still used on freehold or leasehold land. In 1930 there were 30,062 of these, of which 17,800 were on plantations, in the Mandated Territory of New Guinea; 2,000 out of a plantation labour force of 3,000 in the British Solomon Islands; the 200,000

in Sumatra showed a decrease both absolutely and relatively from the earlier figures of the decade; and the 8,000 in Papua have been steady for a long time. All of these indentured labourers are recruited locally, except for a part of those in Sumatra, who were taken from Java; but the French are still indenturing coolies from Annam and Tonkin for labour in New Caledonia and Oceania.

5. An unusual form of land tenure has been evolved in Java, where natives were working smallholdings and sugar companies wanted large areas for planting cane. The companies rent the land from the peasants at £3 to £4 per acre and then pay them for working for the duration of the sugar crop. The law does not permit native land to be rented continuously for more than eighteen months in three years, and the land used for sugar is usually irrigated rice land, which produces in a three-year rotation three or four crops of rice, one of sugar, one of tobacco—which is sometimes also grown by the company—and possibly one green cover crop.

6. In many areas native chiefs have established plantations on their own family land, and obtain labour by their customary power of conscription. The system is found in the Gold Coast, the French Cameroons, Uganda, and the Mandated Territory of New Guinea.

7. In large areas of South and Central America freehold grants to colonists rendered the aborigines landless, and they were then compelled to work on the foreign estates. Usually they cultivate their own food and are paid a low wage, but they are not allowed to dispose of their labour freely. A somewhat similar situation is growing in parts of Africa, where large grants to Europeans have left natives short of land and forced them to live as labour tenants on the plantations.

8. Share-farming, or metayage, was a familiar system of feudal land tenure in both the East and the West. The

landowner divides a large area between several tenant cultivators, who pay rent in the form of a share of the produce; and since the remainder forms their remuneration they bear the risks of production equally with the landowner, which puts them in a different category from the labourer who receives a fixed wage. Whether this system should be classed with plantation or peasant production depends, as we have indicated before, on whether the farmer is left to exercise his own initiative or is guided by a landowner who determines the technical matters of cultivation and provides the capital. In the Philippines, and on native-owned plantations in other places, the former method is found; in the zamindari districts of India the degree of control exercised by the landowner differs, but on the whole he is interested in introducing the most productive methods in order to obtain the maximum rent; where European management has introduced large-scale equipment the labour of native tenants is very carefully directed. The most notable example of such an undertaking is probably the Gezira scheme in the Anglo-Egyptian Sudan, at present the largest cotton producer among colonial areas. The Sudan Plantations Syndicate undertook to finance the settlement of peasant cultivators on about three hundred thousand acres irrigated by the Sennar Dam on the Blue Nile which the Government built. The land was divided into holdings of thirty feddans, so systematically laid out that they could be ploughed and ridged for planting by the Syndicate's tractors. The subsequent cultivation and picking is done by the peasants under the regular supervision of the plantation experts, and the Syndicate takes over the crop for ginning and marketing. The net proceeds are ultimately divided: 35 per cent to the Government for service of the building loan, 25 per cent to the Syndicate, and 40 per cent to the cultivators. Provision was made for modifying the proportions when necessary. From the inception of the scheme there have been surplus applicants for every tenancy, and the Syndicate has successfully launched a subsidiary company on the same lines. Originally there was a three-year rotation of crops, with cotton on ten feddans every year, but this is now being changed to a four-year rotation, and twenty-five thousand feddans added to the total area to maintain the annual yield of cotton.

9. A more widespread form of co-operation between native cultivators and foreign capital is found where the peasants hold their own land, and the foreign management is concerned with supervising and processing the crop. A cotton syndicate was formed on this basis in French Togo, and the Plantations Congolaises undertook to extend the cultivation of foodstuffs in the Belgian Congo by contract with the chiefs. But this method of organization is of most importance in the sugar-cane industry, where the central factories in most of the important exporting areas—Cuba, Fiji, Trinidad, Hawaii, the Philippines, Mauritius—obtain a large proportion, if not all, of their crop by farming agreements with smallholders, whose cultivation is directed by the company's technical experts. Where a plantation owns a larger area than it can cultivate directly with hired labour, e.g. the Colonial Sugar Refining Company in Fiji, it leases small allotments to peasants; but some factories, notably in Cuba, own no land, while others, e.g. Usine St. Madeleine in Trinidad, grinds both its own and peasants' canes. It was by a similar method of contract for delivery that the French introduced indigo into India in rotation with the native food crops. And the British Cotton Growing Association established ginneries in West Africa without owning any agricultural land.

The size of a plantation unit varies widely. We have said already that native cultivation may be regarded as changing from peasant to plantation when the landowner ceases to be a labourer and becomes a manager, and this often involves an area of only fifty to one hundred acres, analogous to the farm in Europe rather than the European plantation in the tropics. The latter ranges from about five hundred to one hundred thousand acres according to the value of the land, the availability of labour, and the nature of the crop. When sugar mills were of small capacity the size of a sugar-cane plantation was three hundred to five hundred acres, but central factories now draw on a growing area of at least five thousand acres, and many of them on much more. Rubber estates which started as a few hundred acres have gradually grown to thousands of acres with greatly improved factory equipment, and large units of banana cultivation are necessary for making full shipments on special vessels. In some other crops—cocoa, coffee, and grains, for example—there is no such pressure to expansion from the more profitable use of machinery. But it is probable that population and labour conditions have had a greater influence on the form and size of plantation organizations than any other factor. It was the problem of labour that caused sugar factories to resort to the method of farming agreements, while a suitable labour supply enables the rubber estates to maintain direct production. Both tea in Assam and coffee in Brazil have been developed wholly by immigrant labour, while in Java indigenous labour was available for these crops as well as others. In other places —Papua, Kenya, Nyasaland—where immigrant labour was not allowed and indigenous was scarce, European holdings have not been developed to their full extent.

Agriculture has to compete for a labour supply with mining in all the African territories—although the competition may be regarded as less the farther the territory is from the mines. In India the plantations recruit in competition with both mining and urban industries; but in Malaya practically all the labour in the mines is Chinese, while on the plantations it is Indian and Javanese as well. Most agricultural wages are day rates based on piecework, but in some places, including all those where indenture is used, the rates are either annual or monthly. Both casual and contract labourers receive food and a small amount of clothing when they live on the plantation, and these and the living conditions are prescribed by the Government in the terms of the contract, but casual daily labourers who live near to their work are usually paid wages only. Large plantations often set aside a small area for the cultivation of foodstuffs by labourers; under the *hacienda* system in Spanish America this was the only means of obtaining food, and in some newer regions it is still the most satisfactory means. The Labour Code of Malaya provides for the allotment of one-sixteenth of an acre per labourer for growing food, and while the tea companies in Assam hold about two million acres, less than one million is under tea. The remainder, which is suitable for rice but not for tea, is cultivated by the labourers. When a garden finds all its land suited to tea, it wants to use it for this crop, and then "there is usually difficulty in keeping labour, who regard a plot of land for their own rice cultivation as essential."[1] On the other hand, rice is still imported for the Indians in Fiji, Mauritius, and Ceylon, and when labour in Africa is taken to a region distant from their home there is sometimes difficulty in getting for them the foodstuffs to which they are accustomed. Such differences all have an influence on the relative attractions of plantation employment as compared with the traditional way of living which we discussed in an earlier chapter.

It is these wide variations in conditions and perquisites that make it impossible to find a basis for comparison for real wages. Hawaii sets an exceptional and unrivalled standard in providing for plantation labourers houses with bathrooms, free fuel, hospitals, day nurseries, and theatres

[1] C. F. Harler, *The Culture and Marketing of Tea*, p. 243.

and baseball clubs;[1] and the fruit companies in Central America have supplied a great deal in the way of hygienic housing, hospital accommodation, and health services, for which employers in Africa waited on the Government—and in some places are still waiting.[2] Compared with such perquisites, the clothing and blankets supplied to East African labourers looks exiguous; but they are munificent in comparison with the one-and-a-half yards of calico yearly bestowed upon the indentured native of New Guinea.[3] And besides these differences, the ruling rate of pay for ordinary manual labour shows wide variations in different territories.

Standard Wage Rates for Unskilled Agricultural Labour[4]

AFRICA

Angola: 6d. daily with food.
Belgian Congo: 2 to 3 francs daily.
French Equatorial Africa: 30 francs monthly with rations.
French West Africa: 3 to 5 francs daily.
Gold Coast: 1s. to 1s. 6d. for general unskilled; little agricultural is employed.
Kenya: 12s. to 20s. monthly for men, 10s. to 12s. monthly for women, with rations.
Mozambique: 5s. to 20s. monthly with rations.
Nigeria: 1s. 6d. to 2s. daily in mining; little hired agricultural labour.
Nyasaland: 5s. to 20s. monthly with rations.

[1] C. A. Barber, "Sugar Cane Economics," *Report of the Imperial Sugar Cane Research Conference*, London, 1931, p. 37.

[2] One of the conditions on which the S.A. des Huileries du Congo Belge was established, however, was that it should provide educational and medical services within its area.

[3] *Pacific Islands Yearbook*, 1932, p. 153.

[4] Collected from the relevant official sources for 1930. In most places there is a wide range of pay for skilled and semi-skilled labour. Except for annual indenture, these rates are no indication of aggregate earnings as the working periods of both contract and casual labour varies widely.

AFRICA—*continued*

Northern Rhodesia: 18s. at urban centres, 5s. in outer districts, monthly with rations.

Southern Rhodesia: 15s. monthly with rations on farms.

Tanganyika: 6s. to 20s. monthly with rations.

Uganda: 6d. to 1s. daily; labourers usually grow their own food.

INDIA

Ceylon: 8 annas per man, 6 per woman, 5 per child daily, with rice. Fixed 1927, reduced 20 per cent after 1930.

India:[1] Average monthly earnings in Assam, Rs. 13–8–7 per man, Rs. 11–1–7 per woman, Rs. 7–8–6 per child. Lower on native plantations in the south.

Indo-China: piastre 0.36, a reduction from 0.38 in 1930, daily with rice.

British Malaya: 40 cents per man, 32 per woman, 16 per child daily with rice in 1930; 20 per cent reduction on immediately preceding years.

Mauritius: 40 to 50 cents daily per man, 30 per woman; increased in the harvest season.

Netherlands East Indies: 6d. to 10d. daily in Java; 10d. in Sumatra.

THE CARIBBEAN

British Guiana: 1s. 3d. to 2s. daily without food.

British West Indies: 1s. to 2s. daily without food.

Colombia: $1 to $1.50 daily by piecework on the banana plantations; average elsewhere 50 cents to $1.

Cuba: $1 to $1.50 daily, before the depression.

THE PACIFIC

British Solomon Islands: £12 per annum with food and housing.

Fiji: Casual, 1s. daily with food; contract, £10 to £12 per annum.

Hawaii: $1 to $1.50 daily, with numerous perquisites.

Mandated New Guinea: 5s. monthly per man, 4s. per boy, with food and housing.

[1] Cmd. 3883, 1931, Chap. XIX.

THE PACIFIC—*continued*

Papua: 10s. monthly with food and housing.
Philippine Islands: 40 to 60 United States cents daily.
Western Samoa: 3s. daily for Chinese contract coolies.[1]

The wide variations in this wage schedule are an indication of the different conditions of demand and supply that prevail in the respective regions. The demand depends upon the extent of natural resources, the amount of development foreign enterprise undertakes, and the capital it introduces. The supply depends upon the situation of the local population with regard to land, whether this is freely accessible, or already excessively subdivided, or arbitrarily appropriated by the Government, and on the excess population in adjacent countries which is available by immigration. The relation of labour productivity to wages in a free market has already been discussed, but it may be opportune to recall at this point that a Government policy of exerting pressure on natives to work at a lower rate than that to which they would voluntarily respond has a direct influence upon the ratio in which the factors of production are combined. With such a policy the marginal substitution of factors is calculated on the expectation that coercion will maintain a low cost labour supply.

It is evident that wages are distinctly higher where labour is employed on a piecework basis, as in Cuba, Hawaii, and the banana plantations of Central America; and even the lower earnings in Malaya compare favourably, when food and housing are considered, with ordinary rates of pay in neighbouring countries. These labourers all work on a wage basis which gives them a direct interest in their productivity; the position of the casual or contract labourer at a fixed

[1] This rate was established with the free contract system in 1923. Under indenture the rate had been 16s. 8d. monthly when the territory was German, and 30s. monthly after it came under British mandate. Roberts, *Population Problems of the Pacific*, p. 288.

time-rate is completely different. "The negro plantation hand takes, in fact, no sort of interest in his job. Its profits do not concern him, neither do its risks. He gets practically the same remuneration whatever crop he is engaged on, and he gets it equally whether the harvest is a success or a failure."[1] It is significant that where employers have made an appreciable capital investment, as in sugar factories and rubber plantations, they should obtain their labour by a form of contract that embodies some measure of incentive to the worker; whereas in other regions, where concessions and land grants represent expectations rather than expenditure on the part of the holders, labour is obtained at low time-rates with considerable official pressure.

Plantation production comprises a series of specialized local cultures, and it has therefore to bear the usual risks that attach to specialization and lack of adaptability to fluctuating demand. This characteristic of the plantation system can be regarded from two standpoints: that of its effect upon particular producing units, and that of its influence upon the fortunes of the political entity of which the plantations are a part. The particular crop cultivated in any place is that which offers the most profitable use for the available factors of production. Since the amount of capital may be regarded as flexible, the deciding factors are land and labour. Thus in some countries—Colombia, Ceylon, and Java, for instance—there is a zonal diversification according to climatic conditions. Bananas in the first, and rubber and coconuts in the other two, growing near sea-level, while coffee and tea grow at higher altitudes; and in Nigeria variations in rainfall between the coast and the northern districts are responsible for belts of different cultures. There are a few regions in which soil and climate combine to form conditions peculiarly suited to a single crop. Examples of these are coffee on the Santo Paulo

[1] Sir Hector Duff, *Cotton Growing in Nigeria*, 1921.

plateau of Brazil and cocoa on the hot sheltered mountain slopes of Ecuador. But natural conditions are in general suitable in most places for more than one crop, and scientific cultivation has done a great deal in recent years to improve natural yields. We find, however, that, in spite of these opportunities for diversification, most large-scale producing areas are dominated by one important crop. The agricultural fortunes of Brazil depend largely on coffee, in spite of an unparalleled range of climate suitable for other crops; coconuts in Malaya are subsidiary to rubber, as pineapples are to sugar in Hawaii; and tobacco in Cuba does not compare in importance with sugar. In the few places where the natural opportunities for diversification are utilized, the reason is to be found either in an unusually plentiful labour supply, e.g. in Java, and to a lesser extent in Ceylon, or in a Government policy of encouragement of multi-culture irrespective of comparative costs, which is the basis of recent cultivation in the Belgian Congo and French West Africa; while the Philippines grow sugar under the shelter of the United States tariff, although they have no comparative advantage in this crop as they have in coconuts and abaca.

From the point of view of the prosperity of a whole territory, it has been claimed that a diversity of cultures gives greater stability than a high degree of specialization, and as far as the secular trend of prices is concerned this is no doubt true. The exchange values of different crops will not all change in the same direction at the same time. But they do all change in this way in times of cyclical fluctuation. The value of exports from Java, the area of most diversified production, was in 1931 only 29 per cent of their value in 1925.[1] Over this period, however, tea had only declined 12·3 per cent in price compared with a decline of 89 per cent in rubber,[2] so that both Java and Ceylon

[1] *Y.C.C.D.*, 1932, p. 228.
[2] *World Agriculture, An International Survey*, p. 94.

were more fortunate than Malaya in having tea as well as rubber. With the assistance of the United States tariff, Philippines centrifugal sugar suffered a fall of only 8 per cent in price between 1929 and 1931, although the decline in world price was three times as much; but abaca, which was dependent on the world market, fell 46 per cent in the same period.[1]

The position of the separate producing units in relation to specialization of culture and fluctuations in price rests upon the question of costs of production. The plantation chooses that crop in the first place which is expected to be most profitable in the existing conditions of demand. When these conditions change, costs of production become a matter of the alternative uses of the factors. From the point of view of cyclical fluctuations, both land that is under a permanent crop and land used for a revenue crop which is part of an established rotation is a specific factor. It has no alternative short-term use. When the secular trend of a particular crop is involved, however, it is sometimes possible to substitute a new and relatively profitable crop for the one that has declined in value. Thus much of the area originally under coffee has been replanted with tea in Ceylon and with rubber in Malaya; and some of that under indigo in India with sugar; while some of the West Indian islands replaced sugar with cotton and arrowroot. And, still more recently, the decline in the price of rubber has caused attention to be directed to the increase of oil palms in Malaya.

While separate plantations in the same area grow different crops, either because of the suitability of their land or, as was indicated above, because it is Government policy to encourage such diversification, the individual plantation remains a highly specialized unit. Evidently the profits of

[1] *Report of the Department of Agriculture and Natural Resources*, Manila, 1931.

concentrating on a single crop, in which there is with the available factors of production the greatest comparative advantage to the producers, are more attractive than the prospect of aiming at the slightly higher degree of stability which might be secured by spreading the risk over a large number of crops. The position of the individual producing unit in relation to the diversification of crops is clearly different from that of the agricultural region as a whole. The latter may benefit to some extent from spreading the risk of fluctuations over a variety of crops. But the plantation is organized primarily to secure the economies of specialization, and as these have become applicable on an increasingly large scale the cost of production has steadily diminished. The most profitable size for a particular unit varies, of course, according to the crop and the natural conditions that influence production, and the rate of profit will in any case depend upon the ability of differing kinds of management. The measure of their success is not the prevention of price fluctuations of their products, but the adjustment of their cost structure to changes in the level of prices.

The essential purpose of plantation development has been to provide exports from the tropics. In some areas it has remained mostly distinct from indigenous economy, in others it has largely replaced the previous forms of native occupation; but everywhere it has in some degree substituted an economy of money exchange for one of self-sufficiency. Besides producing exports, plantations usually require a large amount of imports. Their capital equipment and working supplies have to be obtained from outside, and to the extent that the labourers do not produce their own food this has to be imported. Hence one characteristic of a plantation area is an extensive foreign trade, and this has sometimes been interpreted as evidence of the greater "prosperity" of this system of production as compared with areas still worked by native methods.[1] But in fact exports —or the lack of them—cannot be used as a measure of the prosperity of a community which is not organized for producing them; this may be consuming what it produces internally without feeling any sense of want. Still less can trade figures be taken to indicate a "greater efficiency of output" by the plantation system. Indigenous economy may be quite as efficient in reaching the ends to which its effort is directed, although these are not included in the trade returns. We do find, however, that with increasing contact with foreign capitalism many native communities have been attracted by the ends of plantation production—that is, they grow revenue crops for export instead of devoting all their effort to producing foodstuffs. But while this form of organization makes them the competitors of plantations in the international market, it does not enable their relative productivity to be compared through export figures. The only significant basis of comparison between the two systems is in their respective costs of production and their capacity to meet given conditions of demand. The position of the plantation with regard to specialization of product and specificity of factors we have indicated above; in order to assess the comparative costs of peasant production we must examine the methods by which the natives organize their exchange economy.

[1] This view is stated uncompromisingly by Alleyne Ireland in his *Tropical Colonization*, and later still in *The Far Eastern Tropics*, p. 136. It was advanced more tentatively by L. C. Knowles, *Economic Development of the British Overseas Empire*, Vol. I, p. 186. They compare figures of exports from territories with indentured labour with those from places without such labour—to the detriment of the latter. But as indentured labour was almost entirely engaged in growing exports, food had to be imported for them; in the other places indigenous labour was growing food as well as exports. Another writer, C. Dennery, in *Asia's Teeming Millions*, found that in 1926 Malaya had the highest *per capita* exports in the world. A little later this distinction was claimed for the Falkland Islands by C. F. Jones, *South America*, p. 108. But it is difficult to regard either area as an inspiring example of prosperity.

CHAPTER VII

CONTEMPORARY METHODS OF PRODUCTION

II. PEASANT PRODUCTION

We have already discussed the fact that while indigenous tenure has a wide range of forms, on the whole collectivist ownership of the land predominates with individual rights of cultivation. But at no point did this system imply a theoretical choice between individual and collective ownership as such; land tenure was an integral part of the whole economy, and cultivation was a-capitalistic and personal rights were limited in the same degree that the production system as a whole was a-capitalistic and personal rights in any kind of property were limited by the nature of the property. Where native peoples did not have individual ownership of land, therefore, it was not because they had rejected that type of organization, but because the concept was too alien to the function of land in their economy as a whole to be a subject of choice. Permanent ownership can be of no significance without permanent cultivation, and the site of crops is continually changed; besides, cultivation does not represent an investment of time and labour in the land itself so much as in the crops. Only enough clearing and turning of the soil is done to provide a yield in the immediate future, so that when a cultivator changes his holding he is not losing any contribution which he has made to an increase in future productivity. To the crops which are the product of his own labour, however, he has a clearly recognized right, so much so that a wife may retain a claim to the crops she has planted if she leaves her husband between sowing them and harvest-time.[1] The vesting of

[1] Orde Browne, *Vanishing Tribes of Kenya*, Chap. V, "Land Tenure." And Westermann, *The African To-day*, p. 114, says regarding the fact that all members of a family have their own property, "In this respect an extraordinary individualism has developed within the family."

tribal land in a communal or patriarchal authority secures a certain orderliness in the individual allotments and the continuity of the whole area under tribal control, and these are the functions which it is important that the system of tenure should perform. Through them the individual gets a guarantee of perpetual means of subsistence, which, in the existing conditions, serves a more useful purpose than a permanent claim to a specific piece of land.

But when a change in the conditions of production and transport endow land with a value due either to scarcity or to capital investment, it lays the basis of individual ownership. So that when a self-contained collectivist society converts its economy to a system of exchange, the innovations in the method of cultivation are followed by certain modifications of the form of land tenure. The establishment of a permanent revenue crop means that the cultivator looks beyond a single harvest for a return on his labour; the system of "shifting" becomes unnecessary when rotation introduces a restorative crop, and also ends through the ground being more thoroughly cleared for a permanent crop by the removal of rocks and stumps than was previously customary. Naturally the family that has performed this heavy initial labour is unwilling to let the land pass into other hands, and the producer who has expended his effort with a view to future benefits expects to retain possession of the fruits of his enterprise. In these circumstances personal rights to a specific piece of land become established, and communal tenure is replaced by individual. Moreover, each cultivator now expects to sell such part of his production as he does not consume himself, he has no surplus in the old sense which used to be contributed to the common stock, and so individual property rights extend from the land to its products.

Freehold tenure is as much a teleological aspect of individual production for exchange as communal tenure is of tribal production for consumption. There is a tendency among students of primitive peoples to treat personal land ownership as something like a social tragedy which a little more anthropological knowledge on the part of the administration might have avoided, but these rights are really an inherent factor in a system of individual production for exchange, and if they are not introduced in the first place, a demand for them quickly follows the realization of their possibilities.[1] People of all kinds readily appreciate both the practical benefits and the intangible satisfactions to be derived from personal property rights, whether these come from development within the community or are introduced by foreign contacts. As Sir Henry Maine pointed out, the movement of progressive societies has been uniform in one respect. There can everywhere be traced the growth of individual obligations; and the substitution of the individual for the group as the unit of which the civil laws take account.[2] Up to the present time capitalistic economy has everywhere progressed on the basis of individual initiative and individual responsibility, and it is not strange that it should stimulate these conditions when it replaces the a-capitalistic organization indigenous to the tropics; but it was not necessary for European influences to introduce personal rights, power, or obligations to primitive people. These were already familiar concepts, operative everywhere in some degree. What the development of a capitalist system did was to give them a greatly increased range of operation. By changing the significance of the time factor in culti-

[1] This matter is discussed by Keesing, *Modern Samoa*, Chap. V, "Land Ownership and Custom." One way of maintaining the old social system is to prevent changes in land tenure, but you cannot change the system on the basis of the old tenure. Nothing in the above argument is meant to imply that in introducing freehold tenure, which was often the only kind they understood, the imperial Governments did no injustice to natives who had customary rights on the same land; that is quite a different matter.

[2] *Ancient Law*, p. 168.

vation from short term to long term, it gave a new investment aspect to the use of land and labour, and personal rights that had been satisfied by recurrent allotments now required more permanent guarantees. At the same time land lost its dominant importance as the sole source of livelihood, there was a wider variety of occupations available as a structure of roundabout production arose; and the use of money as a medium of exchange gave land a value similar to that of any other commodity. It lost its old character of the inalienable basis of communal life, and became not only the permanent possession of individuals but a negotiable form of wealth. Under these new conditions the security of the individual rests upon rights of ownership and transfer while under the old it had depended upon communal grants and community rights.

Among West African tribes where communal tenure and shifting cultivation were customary, "cocoa planting has revolutionized the native system of land titles. Where only annual crops were under consideration a short, temporary occupation with subsequent reversion to tribal ownership seemed an adequate provision, but with the establishment of permanent cocoa plantations the planter claimed perpetual and undivided proprietorship."[1] In the French African territories security of tenure is only guaranteed to those natives who register title to their land, there is no recognition of tribal rights, and it is according to the spread of revenue cultivation that individuals have taken steps to obtain titles.[2] Experience in the Belgian Congo seems to

[1] G. C. Dudgeon, op. cit., p. 59. The *Annual Report on Togo*, 1929, also mentions the influence of cocoa cultivation in extending occupancy in that territory. A similar view of the influence of revenue cultivation on tenure is in "Mixed Farming and Peasant Holdings in Tanganyika Territory," A. J. Wakefield, *E.C.G. Review*, April 1934.

[2] Apparently still greater efforts are now being made to facilitate personal ownership in the interests of money crops. "Au moment où nous poussons les indigènes vers les cultures riches, nous devons tendre

have shown that native interest in productive development is allied with rights of ownership, and the method recently advocated by the Duke of Brabant is to permit "l'indigène d'accéder à la propriété individuelle."[1] Uganda provides an unusual example of the introduction of freehold tenure since there the land rights were granted before the cultivation of export crops began. The result has been that on the one hand the chiefs have been eager to encourage a crop from which they could collect a money rent, while on the other the peasants have been anxious to buy land of their own whenever possible, so that there has been a large and rapid increase in the number of smallholdings.[2] In Nyasaland and Northern Rhodesia natives are leaving their tribal land to take up holdings near the towns where they can carry on market-gardening; and it must be the recognition that they are likely to do this which has led to careful regulations for preventing them in Kenya and Southern Rhodesia. Rubber in Malaya and other revenue crops in

. . . à développer chez eux l'instinct de propriété. . . . L'Article 28 de l'arrête du sept. 1926 habilité les chefs de circonscription à octroyer gratuitement des permis d'occuper, de 10 hectares au maximum, à titre individuelle ou collectif sans frais, sans formalité au indigènes méritants. Une fois la mise en culture par cultures riches, réalisée et constatée, la propriété définitive est accordé." *Y.C.C.D.*, 1932, F.E.A., p. 302. And in Indo-China a scheme has been introduced "permettre l'accession rapide à la petite propriété des paysans modestes et serieux." *Y.C.C.D.*, 1930, p. 74.

[1] The Senate, July 25, 1933, reported Congo Revue, *Politique Coloniale*.

[2] Under the Uganda Agreement of 1900, 9,003 sq. miles were allotted to 3,700 owners virtually in freehold. Prior to 1916, 102 sq. miles were sold by native owners to non-natives, but this process has been stopped by law. There is still, however, a great deal of transfer activity between natives, and the number of registered landowners exceeds 10,000. *Colonial Report*, 1930. The figure of 16,000 is given by Mair, op. cit., p. 170, note, 1934. It is significant of the influence of long-term values that a tenant, "on giving up his land, may claim compensation for improvements, such as coffee-trees or a good house with corrugated iron roof and joinery windows," which he has made independently of the landlord. Ibid., p. 170.

Java[1] are grown on land held in individual and family tenure, while the communal village lands of India and Ceylon are almost entirely used for food crops.

Apart from the form of tenure, which can change under the influence of new conditions, the amount of land available for each cultivator varies greatly between different regions and forms an important factor in determining the particular system of exchange economy which is adopted. Besides this there is the question of obtaining a supply of capital, both for increasing productivity and for financing revenue production in the place of subsistence cultivation. And according to the relative supplies of these factors there have developed several methods of converting a self-contained economy to money exchange. The primary method, and the one that requires least from the native in the way of initiative and change, is to work for money in foreign employment while continuing to grow consumption crops at home. The most familiar example of this is the contract labour which leaves the tribal reserves in Africa for occasional periods, but it is also found where natives are only willing to work for a short time outside their communal organization as in Fiji and Papua.

Another method is that of growing revenue crops with or without subsistence and selling them to a mill or merchant. This is found where the Government has directly encouraged independent production on the part of the natives, e.g. the Gold Coast, Nigeria, Uganda, and, recently, the Belgian Congo. And also where there were experienced peasants, interested in benefiting from new opportunities, as in Malaya, the Dutch East Indies, and Ceylon.

The third method is a contract between native landowners and foreign capitalists to supply jointly the labour and

[1] In order to stimulate production the Dutch Government decided in 1913 to transfer land as far as possible from village to individual tenure. S. H. Roberts, *Population Problems of the Pacific*, p. 229.

equipment necessary to work the land by large-scale methods. The most widespread use of this method is the sugar-cane central factory system in all the chief exporting countries, and it has also been very successful in cotton-growing under the Sudan Plantations Syndicate; and has more recently been tried with cotton in French Togo, and cassava in the Belgian Congo.

Finally, the natives can avoid dependence upon foreign capitalists in any capacity by forming co-operative associations to provide the necessary resources for producing and marketing their own crops. But this is a method that requires some knowledge of the processes of exchange economy, and even when a community becomes willing to adopt it the system cannot be established without a measure of Government sympathy and instruction. Real co-operation must be perfectly voluntary, and it is spreading steadily among the cacao producers of the Gold Coast and Nigeria, and the coffee growers in Tanganyika, and has made a beginning in Malaya and Ceylon. The large number of societies in India were for "Better Living," and the improvement of production was only incidental to their aims.[1] Some Governments have introduced a form of compulsory association between native producers in connection with Government banks, which is intended to stimulate thrift and saving, and also provide on a business basis for the credit needs of their production. This method is found in French West

[1] The aims and methods of co-operation among producers with small resources are fully discussed by C. F. Strickland, *Co-operation for Africa*, 1933, where he also indicates the difference of compulsory organization.

The "Report on Rural Credit Systems of Indo-China, Siam, Federated Malay States, and Dutch East Indies" in the *Report of the Governor-General of the Philippine Islands* for 1931, states the agricultural finance methods of these places very fully.

Yearbook of Agricultural Co-operation, 1934, p. 89, Ceylon, describes the difficulties that arise in practice in handling native produce. Page 95, Gold Coast, discusses the saving in middlemen and finance costs that can be effected by the cacao societies.

Africa and Indo-China, while in the Dutch East Indies it was aimed at making the native peasants the debtors of the Government in order to exclude private moneylenders who might gain possession of the land.

At the present time we find several forms of peasant production in the various tropical countries, each form indicating a different degree of subsistence culture and of capitalization.

1. The tribal cultivators of communal lands in Africa and the Pacific, and the village communities of India and the East, show least change in their traditional organization under the influence of foreign commercial contacts; but they have new markets for the sale of their products, and have to some extent learnt improved methods of cultivation. In most of these areas, e.g. East Africa, India, Fiji, the movement in production has been quite voluntary, but in others, e.g. Belgian Congo, Papua, French West Africa, much of the addition to the customary effort of the natives has been imposed by the metropolitan power.

2. Indigenous peasants cultivating individual holdings, which are divided in different proportions between food and money crops, have grown steadily into the most important form of native exchange production. The movement has transformed the economy of the British West African territories and is spreading in French West Africa; it is responsible for most of the cotton from Uganda, and the native rubber from Malaya and Ceylon, while a large proportion of the exports from India and native products in the Philippines are grown by this method.

3. There is also developing a class of smallholders outside their original lands, either stimulated to migrate by overcrowding at home, e.g. the Javanese who go to Sumatra, or attracted by enterprise under new conditions, e.g. natives in Nyasaland and Northern Rhodesia, who leave their

tribal areas to become market gardeners near the new urban centres.

4. In some places Indian immigrants form an "Intermediate Race" between native proprietors and European capitalists, and hold land in freehold or leasehold either from the Government, e.g. Mauritius, British Guiana, Trinidad, and parts of East Africa, or from the native owners, e.g. Fiji.

5. A class of native peasants who live on foreign-owned land as labour tenants or "squatters" has arisen in a few places, e.g. Kenya, Nyasaland, consequent on large European concessions, but they grow almost entirely foodstuffs for themselves and contribute little on their own account to exchange production.

6. Another type of organization to be distinguished in the category of peasant production is that of "share-farmers," a parallel of the metayage system of Europe, who cultivate allotments belonging to a large landowner and hand over to him a prearranged amount of the produce. This system is found in the Philippines[1] and in some parts of South America where the landlord takes no active part in the direction or management of cultivation, although he may supply the capital requirements of the farmers. It is in leaving the initiative and enterprise to the tenant that the system differs from that of plantation cultivation, which is under centralized management. But while "share-farming" represents from the point of view of the cultivator a form of rent payment—made in produce instead of in labour as in the case of "squatters"—and from the point of view of the landlord is a method of renting land, it differs from the ordinary form of tenancy for which a rent is fixed in advance.

7. Finally, there are the rent-paying peasants whom social or legal changes have detached from land of their own.

[1] A detailed account of the organization in the different provinces is given in the *Bulletin of the Bureau of Labour*, Manila, 1929. pp. 107 et seq.

Prominent among these are the tribes in Uganda who lost their old cultivation rights under the Land Settlement and are now tenants of the freehold landlords. In the West Indies this status has arisen because the labouring population was acquired from Africa or India, and so had no original rights in the land; and in some other places natives prefer to pay for living in a desirable area to having land of their own in a less attractive location. The largest aggregation of rent-paying peasants, however, is found in India where the zamindars, originally tax-collectors of the Mogul Emperors and transformed into landlords by British law, collect rent from their tenants, and the Government collects land revenue from the ryots, the cultivating occupants of Crown land.[1] Both zamindari and ryotwari systems, however, also fall within the classes of village communities and indigenous cultivators mentioned above. It is an historical accident that they should be organized on a different revenue basis from the African peoples who came later under European rule, but the organization aimed at using rather than changing their traditional forms and customs.

An indigenous economy has never been converted to exchange production without some degree of instruction or assistance from the foreign Government; wherever a native community is making any change in its system of production there will be found officials and ordinances.[2] The character

[1] Abstract of 1931 Census of India, Cmd. 1494, 1932, gives the following distribution of ownership and labour:

Landlords (non-cultivators) ..	3,257,391
Cultivating owners	27,006,100
Cultivating tenants	34,173,904
Agricultural labourers	31,480,219

[2] "There can be no doubt that at the start the cultivation of cotton in Uganda was due not to any legal compulsion but to moral pressure on the part of the Government and the chiefs." Cmd. 2387, 1925. Explicit directions for exerting this presure have since been given in Tanganyika. "As soon as it is shown to the satisfaction of the Administrative Officer that a body of natives desires to grow economic crops

of governmental intervention, however, may differ greatly. It may be formulated in response to a demand on the part of the natives for instruction or assistance in improving their production; or it may take the opposite form of pressure to make them undertake production which the metropolitan country thinks desirable, and even then the degree of directness of the methods vary considerably. Sometimes it has been sufficient to provide technical supervision for voluntary labour, but more often the direction of native effort has been carefully controlled; and a process that is started by pressure may, of course, develop with enthusiasm if the natives find it profitable. But whatever their attitude may be, their agricultural system is for all practical purposes a Government scheme of development, and in the determination of the scheme fundamentally important issues are involved. Since they are without means of research themselves and are usually remote from markets, the natives are necessarily dependent upon the advice offered

for sale or export he should assist them in every way to do so. If he finds, however, that a particular community turns a deaf ear to his exhortations to them to adopt some active form of work it will be his duty to use every legitimate means at his command to induce them to take up the cultivation of economic crops." *Report on the Recruitment, Employment, and Care of Government Labour, Tanganyika*, 1930, Section 53, (*e*).

In Nyasaland the development of native cotton followed a series of Government Ordinances, and a Tobacco Development Board was established to assist native tobacco. Sessional Paper, 1, 1930, *Report on the Formation of a Native Agricultural Board.*

In Chapter III we discussed the Compulsory Cultivation methods of the Belgian Congo, Papua, and French West Africa. France and Belgium also make provision for improving and assisting voluntary production.

As a general indication of the aim and method of developing native production where direct coercive measures are not applied, we may take the description of Dudgeon, op. cit., p. 41: "The demonstration to the natives of the fact that, by the proper employment of manuring and crop rotation, they would be able to farm the same piece of land for an indefinite number of years. . . . To encourage the natives in the formation of permanent plantations of fruit and other economic trees."

them; they plant the seed they are given, cultivate the area they are told to, and adopt the methods recommended in so far as they can. Hence the responsibility for their fortunes upon the new basis of production lies with the authority which has directed their course.[1] Unless means are found of increasing his total productivity, the cultivation of revenue crops means that the native will grow less of his own food; and the question that arises is whether the value of the new product will be sufficient to compensate for this deficiency by purchase, and to what extent the community should be allowed to become dependent upon exchange supplies for its subsistence. If any people produce for sale instead of consumption by their own choice and initiative they must feel that this course yields the greater reward; but besides the fact that some natives receive a great deal of persuasion in making the choice, very rarely are any of them in a position to anticipate with certainty the reward it will yield. They are changing from stable to unstable conditions; and even if they are eager to obtain purchasing power, backward communities are quite ignorant of the fluctuations of market prices and the instability of an income based on exchange values. On this point, therefore, there are two questions to be considered by the Government. To what extent can the standard of living of the native community safely be allowed to fluctuate with changes in the price of one commodity? And when a really extensive scheme of cultivation is undertaken, what effect will the new supply have upon the existing market price of the product?

[1] The situation with regard to agriculture is under these conditions similar to that which has arisen in the mine area of Northern Rhodesia, and of which the economist on the recent commission of investigation wrote: "Stabilization (permanent separation of the native from his tribal economy) in its completest form is a grave risk unless the Territory is prepared at each succeeding depression to carry more of the responsibility for those who have become urbanized." *Modern Industry and the African*, Part III, "The Economic Problem," E. A. G. Robinson, p. 117.

The answer to the first question depends upon what margin above the subsistence level the productivity of the natives has attained. The commodities they produce are likely to feel the severest effects of a general decline in prices, and the influence of this diminution of income upon the natives' standard of living corresponds to the place it was to fill in their demand schedule. If it prevents them buying bicycles, or even new blankets, although they regret it keenly, the social effects will not be as serious as if it reduces them to starvation by stopping the import of necessary foodstuffs; and most Governments have tried to guard against the latter contingency by maintaining the cultivation of food crops along with the increase in revenue production. It has often been possible to do this by improving the methods of soil utilization so as to give a more productive mixture or rotation of crops without appreciably increasing the total labour of the cultivator; in other places where the production of food did not already require all the native's time, a revenue crop has been made an extension of his activity instead of a substitute occupation. But it may sometimes be difficult to maintain this balance where the size of individual holdings is limited, and a permanent crop becomes attractive. In British Malaya, for instance, at the time of the rubber boom the peasant preferred to buy imported rice and put his land under rubber, and the Government refused to lease for rubber growing any more land that was suitable for rice. At that time the peasant could see a net advantage in expending all his time on a money crop, but it was an advantage that did not last; and only natives who had other means of support could cease tapping when the sharp fall in prices occurred. Production for the commodity market is always a speculation in future prices, and the native cannot afford to gamble with his food supply. But if he is to be protected from destitution through ill-advised enterprise in the early stages of his capitalistic career, it is equally important that he should not permanently rely on the intervention of a paternalist Government to save him from the unfortunate consequences of his own inertia or initiative.[1] In seeking the advantages of money exchange, he must learn to reckon with its liabilities also, and the chief of these is a change in the barter terms of trade against the commodity he produces.

In extending the cultivation of export crops administrative authorities do not appear to have given as much attention to the relation of these new supplies to market conditions as they have given to the maintenance of native food crops. Yet since this is really a question of ability to sell a product that is grown for sale, it should have as important a place as anything else in the preliminary consideration of the distribution of the native's effort between final ends. It is, at the least, disappointing to the peasant to find that the more produce he grows, the less money he gets;[2] and the accumulation of unsold stocks may prove a serious embarrassment to the Government. Some peasant cultivation has expanded because a certain product proved a "good native crop," e.g. cacao in the Gold Coast, and the Government wanted the population to get money for buying imports; or a suitable crop for natives may be introduced for the same reason where there is no likelihood of an exchange economy being established by foreign investment, e.g. cotton and cacao in Nigeria along with increased production of palm oil; where there was already a skilled peasant population, the natives adopted any new crop introduced

[1] This point is discussed in the *Report on Cotton Growing in Nigeria*, Duff, p. 56, "Guaranteed Prices."

[2] Dr. Mair, in *An African People in the Twentieth Century*, says of cotton-growing by the Baganda, "Most natives believe that the price is fixed by the Government, and that when it is low they are being deliberately oppressed," p. 151. And Marcossen, in *An African Adventure*, p. 180, mentions the reluctance of Congo natives who had gathered ivory with the idea that the price was high to sell it when they returned to the coast and found the price had fallen.

by plantations that seemed profitable, notably rubber in the East Indies and Malaya; and a very important reason for the encouragement of much of the native cultivation of the present time is the same as that which led to the early establishment of plantations, the desire of each imperial Power to obtain commodity supplies which it did not itself produce from an area which was under its control. This desire has been largely inspired by the hope of profit, for until large-scale production reduced them to the same market status as wheat and potatoes the commercial products successively discovered in the tropics—spices, sugar, tea, rubber—were highly valued; but an even more influential factor in recent years has been the autarchic policy of avoiding dependence on foreign sources of supply of any kind, a policy which is most conspicuously exemplified in colonial affairs by the "counterpart-to-the-metropole" scheme of production which France has since the war been fostering in her tropical territories. Under such a scheme comparative costs of production become of secondary—if any—importance, and concomitantly with assistance in the increase of production the metropolitan Government sets up a system of duties and taxes which brings the colonial exports to the home market instead of letting them go elsewhere,[1] keeps products of alien origin out of the home market for the benefit of colonial producers, and finally

[1] This method of directing trade is a feature of assimilation policy. It imposes a general export tax which is rebated on shipments to the metropolitan market. The advantage which accrues to the producer depends upon the extent of that market. If he grows more than it can absorb, the export tax increases the cost of selling in a foreign market. But he only enjoys a price advantage in the home market if there is an import duty on the same commodity from foreign sources. Then the question of the elasticity of home demand arises. The higher price may reduce consumption, and thus limit colonial production. Assimilation policy, however, is safeguarded from criticism on such grounds by claiming as its objective reciprocity of exchange between the colonies and the metropole, and not maximization of production.

subsidizes the sale of surplus production which has to be made below cost in the open market.

Such an elaborate method of counteracting the forces of world competition can only be sustained as an integral part of national policy, but with the exception of Belgium[1] and Holland all the imperial Powers provide some degree of tariff protection for the products of their tropical territories in their respective markets. The catastrophic effect of the Civil War in the United States on the textile industry in England made even a Free Trade era realize the danger of being wholly dependent on foreign sources for vital supplies, and a bad crop in 1904, which put Lancashire on short time, gave an impetus to cotton-growing within the Empire to which the last war added new vigour.[2] Many tropical products—tea, sugar, cacao, coffee, tobacco—were already subject to revenue duties, and in 1919 an imperial Preference rate of 25 per cent to 66 per cent reduction on the general tariff was introduced; and in 1932 the preferential duty was also extended to citrus fruits, bananas, and rice, and a new subsidy for sugar established. The United States admits the products of the Philippines, Porto Rico, and Hawaii free of duty; and there has in consequence been an enormous expansion of production since they came under United States control. These measures have had the effect of making colonial produce saleable when the home market could absorb it, while the same crop from other regions has been carried over from one year to the next. Philippines sugar finds a market in the United States, for instance, and sugar from British colonies finds one in England, while Java and Cuba, where the cost of production is lower, hold unsold stocks; but apart from the fact that some

[1] Prevented by the Congo Basin Convention of the Treaty of Berlin, 1885.

[2] A full account of the development is given in *Cotton in British West Africa*, N. M. Penzer, published by the Federation of British Industries.

commodities, e.g. rubber, abaca, oil seeds, are largely dependent on a foreign market, no measure has been devised for protecting colonial producers from a general decline in prices.[1]

And besides cyclical fluctuations, a large increase in production is likely to cause a steady downward trend in secular prices.[2] Conditions do sometimes occur in which the elasticity of demand for a commodity is greater than unity; for instance, when the industrial uses of rubber were expanding in the first decade of this century. But such a situation does not last indefinitely, and the price falls rapidly as soon as the expansion of production exceeds that of demand. A diminution in the native's returns on his production can then be avoided only if his costs are reduced proportionately to the fall in prices and his output sufficiently expanded to maintain the income which he had expected to obtain from revenue production. The need of this ultimate adjustment to market conditions is a probability

[1] Comparative table of price decline and changes in production, *World Agriculture*, p. 94, shows the following conditions in tropical products:

CROP	PERCENTAGE FALL IN PRICE, AUGUST 1931 OVER 1925–29	CHANGES IN WORLD PRODUCTION IN 1931 OVER 1925–29
Rubber	89	+ 21
Hemp	60	− 10
Cotton	58·9	+ 2
Maize	56·6	− 3
Jute	55·4	− 46
Rice	43	+ 3
Coffee	41·1	+ 10
Sugar	27·7	—
Tea	12·3	+ 1

[2] It must also be remembered in this connection that tropical products are affected by changes in supply from other areas. Beet and cane sugar are a familiar example, but it was the relative scarcity of animal fats which first stimulated the production of oilseeds for foodstuffs in Europe.

which a sound scheme of production in any form must keep in view. Plantations, however, are in a position to do their own anticipating as to costs and prices, while natives at the beginning of an exchange economy have no means of judging the course of fluctuations, so that this responsibility falls on the authority which directs native production. Most Governments, we have seen, provide protective tariffs for colonial produce and some of them grant subsidies to colonial producers; but while these may supply a welcome margin over competitive world costs, or a palliative for unprofitable transitional conditions, they are not a means of permanently valorizing a commodity against the trend of the barter terms of trade. The only criterion of development for any sound system is the earning-power of the innovations it introduces, and not the artificial control of the price of their product,

An indication was given in the last chapter of the issue that has gradually risen to prominence with the increasing production of peasant crops in competition with plantation—namely, that of the comparative costs of the two systems. Recent discussions of the subject reveal two opposite and conflicting views of the nature of the native's costs of production. One is that "the smallholder can afford to tap or not as suits him, while continuous output is virtually forced upon the plantation company whatever the state of the market, owing to the piling up of overhead charges."[1] Against this, in reference to the same smallholders, is the statement that they have to sell whatever prices may be, and "costs do not enter into their calculations in the same way as they do for plantations."[2] We have already discussed plantation costs, and in comparing them with peasant costs two points arise: that of relative cheapness under given conditions of demand,

[1] *Report on the Visit of the Under-Secretary of State for the Colonies to Ceylon and Malaya*, 1927, Cmd. 3235, 1928.

[2] *Report of the Department of Agriculture of British Malaya*, 1929.

and that of elasticity of supply in relation to fluctuating prices.

As an independent producer the native's costs of production are "opportunity costs," and they can only be measured by the alternative uses of his land and labour in terms of real income. From the standpoint of relative cheapness this means that it will pay the peasant to cultivate a crop in which the large scale method of the plantation has a comparative advantage, or of which he can produce only an inferior quality, as long as there is no more profitable form of cultivation available to him. From the standpoint of elasticity of supply it means that if falling prices for a revenue crop reach a stage at which he would derive greater satisfaction from expending his effort upon direct production for consumption than upon obtaining purchasing power, he will change from the latter to the former. Hence the degree of elasticity of native production depends upon two factors: the alternative uses for which the land of smallholders is suitable, and the attractions for the cultivators of the alternative ends that are satisfied by different forms of production. These all vary according to the different conditions under which natives carry on revenue production. If they have been buying imported food, it might easily be better to revert to home-grown when the barter terms of trade turn against them; but on the other hand the wants which they have acquired dependent upon purchasing power may prove inelastic in terms of effort, and it would be worth while to sacrifice some additional food cultivation in order to continue going to the cinema regularly or to obtain tyres for a valued bicycle.

The limits within which production can be adjusted must, however, depend upon how specific a factor the particular piece of land involved is. If a peasant has his holding completely under a money crop, and no alternative means of subsistence is accessible to him, then he "has to sell whatever market prices may be," and his costs of production are identical with a minimum level of subsistence.[1] But if the cultivation of food crops has accompanied his extension of revenue production, then "the smallholder can afford to tap or not as suits him." For some other crops, however, this statement must take a somewhat different form than it does for rubber. Cacao pods must be picked when they are ripe or the tree will be injured, while latex can be left untapped to the benefit of the tree. If the cacao farmer intends to preserve his crop, therefore, he must continue picking and then decide if the price is sufficient to warrant cleaning and fermenting the beans. Where the native crop is copra, the coconuts can be left to fall when they are ripe, and the only labour involved is for cutting and drying the copra. To an even greater extent than in the case of rubber, the supply of this crop depends upon the inducement which the market price offers in the short run. Still another situation arises when the revenue crop is one of an established rotation for which there is no immediate substitute, which is the position of most native cotton at the present time. The profitability of such a crop is not to be judged by its money yield alone, but also by its relation to the rotating crops, and it is likely that the supply will be maintained until the price falls so low that it becomes preferable to fallow the land rather than to pick the crop. The point at which such a choice would become effective depends, of course, upon the elasticity of demand for income

[1] The relation of this aspect of peasant cultivation to large-scale mechanization is comprehensively stated in *World Agriculture*, p. 279, letter from Mr. A. P. McDougall: "A superficial view would tend to indicate that production on these lines would kill the teeming millions of peasant cultivators in other parts of the world. Such a conclusion leaves out of account the staying-powers of civilizations based on peasant life. These are the only people in the world who can survive war, pestilence, and financial disaster. Their standard of living may be reduced to a level incredibly low, but they still survive and produce their crops."

which we discussed above; the more difficult it is to dispense with wants that require purchasing power, the less will production contract when prices fall. In fact, it is conceivable that the wants characteristic of a money economy may become so fixed that an extra effort will be made to satisfy them with a falling price level by marketing more produce, but adjustment in this direction requires some scope for further productivity on the part of the peasant, either by an increase of area or an improvement of method. We argued above that it was the responsibility of a Government which stimulated peasant production to provide for such an adjustment to the secular trend of prices. And where this is done the concept of a standard of living basis of costs has a completely different connotation from that which resists plantation competition by an "incredibly low" subsistence level. With regard to cyclical fluctuations, however, the problem of a long-term alteration of cultivation does not arise. The situation simply is that if the native can provide all the consumption goods he wants by direct production, he is able to cease revenue cultivation when he feels it is not worth while; but if he has become to an appreciable extent dependent upon purchasing power for subsistence, and has no better short-term alternative, then he must continue to market his crop.

Information as to the effect which the depression since 1929 has actually had on native production is scanty and incomplete, but there is sufficient to be of significance in connection with the preceding theoretical analysis. The native producers of rubber in the Netherlands East Indies curtailed their production most markedly in response to the fall in price; the smallholders in Malaya showed a smaller reduction, since more of them were dependent upon that crop for a livelihood;[1] but the plantation output in both

[1] Figures from the *Thirteenth Report on Native Rubber Cultivation* by the Department of Agricultural Economics, N.E.I., reprinted *Bull. R.G.A.*,

countries showed almost no change.[1] In the Netherlands Indies it is stated that "the population has shown much disinterestedness for the cultivation of crops yielding commercial produce, while in almost every province the attention has all the more been attracted to the rearing of foodstuffs and that of second crops of fruit and flowers."[2] Shipments of groundnuts from India decreased because the peasants preferred to eat their nuts rather than sell at the prevailing low prices;[3] and in spite of Government efforts to get more of this product planted in Senegal after the short crops of 1931 and 1932, the natives, "seeing their greater efforts rewarded with a smaller monetary return, are becoming inclined to sow for their personal wants rather than for pecuniary gain. Millet and manioc are thus beginning to replace the groundnut in their fields."[4] Similarly, in Gambia, where groundnuts had been the only crop and rice imported for food, the cultivation of local foodstuffs was introduced. In the Mandated Territory of New Guinea the natives are accustomed to producing practically all

April 1933. The percentage change in rubber production in 1932 as compared with 1929 was:

N.E.I. Estate	101·5	Native 57·5
B. Malaya Estate	98·0	Native 85·0
Ceylon, total exports	61·5	
Other countries	54·5	
World percentage of 1929 ..	83·5	

The last group of countries comprise mostly native holdings, therefore, except in Ceylon, where many plantations have old trees, "it is mainly the native rubber cultivation which has contributed to the restriction of production," p. 230.

[1] The same trend of production is shown by palm oil. Except from the Belgian Congo, where output is largely plantation, exports from West Africa, i.e. native production, declined from 1931 to 1933. But the effect of this on the world market was more than compensated by the plantation increase from Malaya and Sumatra.

[2] *Y.C.C.D.*, 1932, p. 209.

[3] *Oilseed, Oil and Oilcake Markets in 1932*, F. Fehr & Co.

[4] "Economic Conditions in French West Africa, 1931–33," *D.O.T. Report*, 562.

they want to consume, and in 1931 "there was a large decrease in the quantity of copra produced by the natives, ascribable mainly to the low price offered for the commodity, the reasons for which were unintelligible to the natives."[1]

In contrast with all these crops, cacao and cotton, the two spectacular successes of native production in Africa, have everywhere maintained the level of production which they had reached before 1930 and in some places have continued to expand. The Uganda cotton crop of 294,000 bales for the season 1932–33 was the largest yet produced, and in Nyasaland there has been a steady increase in native cultivation, while plantation has sunk to negligible proportions.[2] These are examples of a revenue crop in conjunction with food crops which meet a definitely established need of purchasing power. Some of the large cacao farmers of the Gold Coast and Nigeria have given up cultivating foodstuffs and depend wholly on their revenue crop, but the holdings of these are so large that they belong to the plantation and not the peasant category of productive organization.

In the light of their respective conditions of production, we may agree that even when a decline in prices diminishes his purchasing power the native producer "is still in a stronger position than the European planter who relies upon his annual profits to meet heavy capital and overhead charges."[3]

[1] *Report on the Mandated Territory of New Guinea for 1932*. This statement has a direct bearing on the point we previously discussed of the Government's responsibility for introducing price conditions which the natives would not at first adequately understand, but the factor which causes production to be curtailed when prices fall is not that the native finds the fall unintelligible, but that he finds the reduced payment unattractive.

[2] *Report of the British Cotton Growing Association for 1933*. Figures of production for the preceding ten years in all areas except India are regularly printed in the *Empire Cotton Growing Review*. It is notable that this increase has taken place without any artificial price encouragements. In the Belgian Congo, where the Government has undertaken to guarantee a price and market for native cotton, the results on production have not been more marked.

[3] "Agricultural Development in Nigeria," P. H. Lamb, *J.A.S.*, April 1933.

But a necessary qualification of this position which is frequently overlooked is that share capital is not a fixed charge on which interest must necessarily be paid.

Besides the question of the comparative costs and productivity of peasant and plantation methods there remains a more general point of view which has given rise to much discussion, that as to which system of production is a better method of developing a new country. Clearly a great deal of the opinion on such a subject is entirely political, and the question of the social status and disabilities of natives as such do not concern us here. A quite separate matter, however, is that of how much initiative in undertaking new development peasants are likely to show in comparison with plantations; and secondly, what measure of stability the economy of a large number of small producers is likely to have in comparison with that of a few large employing units.

It was not until a late stage of imperial history that the possibilities of economic progress through entirely native enterprise was recognized, and as we have already seen, this form of development is a characteristic of twentieth-century policy. The leading exposition of its advantages is found in the Address of the Governor to the Legislative Council of Nigeria in 1920, "Agricultural interests in tropical countries which are mainly or exclusively in the hands of the native peasantry have, firstly, a firmer root than when owned and managed by Europeans, because they are natural growths and not artificial creations and are self-supporting as regards labour, while European plantations can only be maintained by some system of organized immigration or by some form of compulsory labour; secondly, they are incomparably the cheapest instrument for the production of agricultural produce on a larger scale than has yet been devised; and thirdly, they are capable of a rapidity of expansion and a progressive increase of output that beggar every record of the past, and are altogether unparalleled in all the long history of European agricultural enterprise in the tropics."[1] By every practical test, therefore, rate, cheapness, and stability of development, peasant production would have a superiority over plantation production. Nevertheless, arguments are still advanced for subjecting native economy to European control. The basic one is that the native will not respond to the advantages of improving his production with sufficient rapidity if left to himself, and must therefore be organized by some external authority who has an interest in making improvements.[2] In the light of the immense expansion of native cacao in West Africa and native cotton in East Africa, as well as native rubber in the East, this appears to be an extremely hazardous hypothesis. Moreover, it is difficult to find a product at the present time enjoying the favourable market situation in which "development from within cannot keep pace with the insistent demand."[3] There is instead an over-supply of most commodities, and the increase of native production is frequently blamed for it. What is true, however, is that in order to produce for the international market the native needs a certain amount of technical instruction in improving the productivity of his methods, and probably also requires some new capital, a factor which it is difficult to increase under the subsistence conditions of indigenous economy. Our foregoing survey of the contemporary forms of production shows that these requirements have been met

[1] Sir Hugh Clifford, *Minutes of the Proceedings of the Council, S.P.*, 1920.

[2] Martin Leake, *Land Tenure and Agricultural Production in the Tropics*, 1927, and "Studies in Tropical Land Tenure," *Journal of Tropical Agriculture*, October 1932–April 1933, probably gives the most technical form of this opinion. He advocates a form of "vertical co-operation" or "triple partnership" which would introduce an active agent between the peasant and the Government, and adduces the success of the zamindari system in India as evidence of the influence of such a third partner in stimulating the effort of the cultivator.

[3] Leake, *Land Tenure and Agricultural Production*, p. 74.

in different ways. In a great many places the Government has organized agricultural services for assisting and advising the natives on technical matters, and has also instituted some form of rural credit for facilitating the acquisition of capital equipment. In other places buying merchants found it in their interest to demonstrate to the natives the profits that could be obtained by improving the methods or quality of their crop; and foreign capitalists have also provided factories or ginneries where it was likely that native produce would be obtained in sufficient quantity for processing. Without disturbing native ownership of land, or introducing the need of compulsory labour, every requisite of efficient market production has been supplied. Tropical people, in fact, have proved eminently amenable to the two fundamental conditions of capitalistic economy—wanting and waiting.[1]

Where there are large areas of land that the indigenous population is clearly inadequate for developing, the introduction of the plantation system bears a different aspect, but the very fact that population is small means that labour will be scarce. Thus the plantations in Malaya and Ceylon,

[1] C. N. French, *Report on the Cotton-Growing Industry in Uganda, Kenya and the Mwanza District of Tanganyika*, 1925, says, "it is no small achievement to have induced them to grow a crop which they cannot eat." Voluntary exchange, of course, follows the multiplication of wants.

And P. H. Lamb, "Agricultural Development in Nigeria," *J.A.S.*, April 1931, says that the success of cocoa in West Africa refutes the early idea that the African would not wait more than a year for a return on his crops. Regarding what might be called the entrepreneurial element, in which the argument for European intervention contends that the native is deficient, we might consider the course of development of the Gold Coast cocoa industry. About 1879 a native trader brought some seed from Fernando Po and made a small plantation in Volta River district. The first crops were said to have been sold to other natives at £1 per pod, and in 1891 the first shipment of 80 lb., valued at £4, was made. It was in 1876 that the first Para rubber seedlings were sent to plantations in Ceylon and Malaya. Is it possible to distinguish between the quality of enterprise shown in the two places?

Sumatra and Fiji, depend almost entirely on immigrant labour; and when it is not practicable to introduce an alien race, as in French Equatorial Africa and the Belgian Congo, plantation cultivation can only be conducted in the place of peasant cultivation, and probably only with some measure of coercion. Until it actually happens, therefore, that an urgent demand for some product arises which native enterprise definitely refuses to satisfy, we cannot refute the judgment that "wherever the system of native cultivation is practicable (as it is in Nigeria) and wherever it is adequately guided, instructed, and encouraged, it will effect more in the long run—it will open up a country more widely, thoroughly, and economically—than would be possible in any other way."[1]

Foreign plantations can in a short time work wonders in a wilderness if they make a sufficient capital outlay. But this rapid development is no guarantee that their ultimate achievement will be equally superior to the capacity of the natives. Against the fact that the training of peasants may be a slower process, and also involves some measure of Government expense, must be set the large investment made by the plantation, probably with a high proportion of fixed charges, which results in a lack of adaptability to long-term market trend. Secondly, an aspect of the plantation system which seems to be ignored in most comparative discussion is the limitation that its cost structure or labour difficulties may set to the development of territorial resources. The experience of New Guinea and Borneo do not suggest that there is any inherent principle of vitality in plantation methods as such. And if natives are to be criticized for making inefficient use of their land, we must consider whether the unploughed areas of Kenya and Nyasaland land grants and the empty spaces on *haciendas* in America are to be exempt from criticism.

[1] *Cotton Growing in Nigeria*, Report of Sir Hector Duff, 1921.

CHAPTER VIII

CONCLUSION

THE acquisition of tropical products was among the earliest ventures of European capitalism, and the spectacular success of its purpose has been achieved by varying methods in the course of many stages of experimentation and development. What is there to be said of the results in relation to the producers of these commodities? In the course of four centuries the extension of the production system of Europe to the remotest coconut groves of the Pacific and the densest forests of Amazonia has brought people of all races and of every type of indigenous economy within the scope of a capitalistic system of exchange which originated in the peculiar conditions of one small group of countries. However large or small has been the degree of success with which this system has pursued its ends in backward regions, it has impressed something of its aims and methods upon the people with which it has dealt. It has supplied the products of blast furnaces in place of hand-made tools, brought foreign textiles to the wearers of skin and bark, and taught the former cultivator of communal foodstuffs to watch the price of market crops with keen individualist interest. Strangely incompatible with the professions of humanitarian intent that have invariably accompanied the process of penetration into backward civilizations, some of these methods may be. But where the native has survived the early onslaught of progress or of enslavement, although he may frequently dislike the terms on which he has been forced to participate in a money economy, he has never rejected the satisfactions that money can provide. Where objections to foreign "exploitation" are made, they are based on the smallness of the profit that accrues to the native, not on the introduction of an exchange economy as such. Limited in particular choices by the smallness of his income, and influenced, perhaps, by standards of satisfaction unfamiliar in Europe, "the native" is nevertheless willing to pursue those ends alien to his indigenous economy of self-sufficiency, and adopted from the wider possibilities of capitalism, of producing to sell and buying to consume.

At the close of a survey of the conditions and methods responsible for this outcome, the question naturally arises as to whether indigenous people have shown any preference for the particular means by which these new ends are to be attained. That is to say, what trend of assimilation to capitalist economy is there discernible in the course of development of backward regions? Under the free working conditions that are supposed to have succeeded the abolition of slavery, there are three methods of adopting an exchange economy:

1. To be completely identified with foreign enterprise as wage-earners.
2. To be completely separated from it as independent producers.
3. To co-operate on a free contractual basis as producers of raw material for foreign-owned factories.

In the distribution of these various forms of occupation there have been very distinct chronological and geographical influences. It is unnecessary to recount here the reasons why the plantation system of the West Indies was not also established in India; why the development of West Africa has followed completely different lines from that of Ceylon; and why still more recently East Africa should give rise to problems and expedients from which Malaya is free. Two things are clear in retrospect. That imperial policy has been based on different hypotheses as to both native characteristics and Governmental responsibility; and that the former differ widely enough for even an identical policy to show different results.

From the standpoint of European enterprise in the tropics, the trend of assimilation of exchange economy by the natives is of direct importance. At the present time the first of the forms of occupation summarized above is identified, as far as agriculture is concerned, with plantation employment, and the plantation is now found under three sets of conditions. It continues in those places where European landowners and a landless working class were the outcome of the abolition of slavery, e.g. in the West Indies, Mauritius, and British Guiana. Secondly, it is found where foreign investors were anxious to undertake a particular culture, and a supply of immigrant labour was available, e.g. in Ceylon, Malaya, Sumatra, and Assam. And thirdly, plantations have been more recently established where Government policy favours the activities of European landowners and endeavours to stimulate a supply of indigenous labour, e.g. in Kenya, the Belgian Congo, French Equatorial Africa, and Mozambique. This indicates that only to a minor extent, and then with frequent complaint and friction, does the system exist in conjunction with a landowning indigenous labour supply. And even in the West Indies, British Guiana, Mauritius, and Fiji, peasant holdings have increased as non-indigenous labour drifted away from plantation employment.

The second form of occupation, that of independent producers for export, is a comparatively new phenomenon in imperial relations with tropical peoples. Producers for consumption purposes, of course, there were in indigenous societies, and the first use which foreign companies or Governments made of them was to exact levies for export. The peasant selling on his own account emerged eventually from the peculiar conjuncture of a land tax based on a misunderstanding of the pre-existing system of tenure in

India; of a need for rehabilitating an economy exhausted and disorganized by extortion in Java; and of an expanding demand for cacao and a climate prohibitive of European enterprise in the Gold Coast. These all served to show that a free native peasantry was a perfectly possible basis of successful development; and where there are not for any reason conflicting European interests, it has now become Government policy to stimulate native producers just as definitely as wage labour in other areas is stimulated. In places where this effort has aroused a large response, a successful beginning in co-operative schemes of providing capital for native producers and marketing their crop has also been made. And this movement naturally raises the question of whether the native will soon be able to supplant the foreign entrepreneur also in the sphere of finance, and completely control local production.

The answer to this question—in so far as an answer can be found without venturing into the field of pure prophecy—lies in the third method by which we found tropical society adopting an exchange economy. Co-operation between the native producer of raw material and the European factory that manufactures it is another comparatively recent phase of imperial relationships, not only in regions which were being newly developed, e.g. Nigeria and Uganda, but as a modification of the pre-existing wage system in other places, e.g. the old "sugar islands." Some crops, e.g. sugar, tea, and sisal, need more capital than the native farmer of three to ten acres can provide for a start; and when foreign investors have provided it, the necessity of maintaining a supply of raw material makes it desirable to secure the direct interest of the labourers in the complete process of production. For other crops, e.g. cotton and coffee, the capital is within the reach of a well-organized scheme of co-operation; but if outside investors are ready to provide it, as they have been in most territories, the growers would only need to undertake this stage of production themselves if they felt that there were more profits or greater marketing facilities to be derived from doing so.

It is unfortunate that no comprehensive data is available of the relative trend of money wages in conjunction with various schemes of compulsion and without them, and of independent native production. There are, as we have seen, an extremely wide range of components of real wages in the form of different food, clothing, housing, and leisure-time recreations, for which it is impossible to formulate an index of comparison; while on the side of independent production there are other elements, both material and psychological, that are not quantitatively commensurable with wage rates. It is possible, for instance, that in the days of great prosperity on the sugar plantations the slaves in the West Indies were better fed than many of their race living—then and now—in the freedom of African forests, but that could not be interpreted as an inducement to a voluntary supply of slaves. And there are similar discrepancies, although probably less in degree, between the conditions of different forms of employment to-day. What it would be significant to have is an index of the relative productivity of labour in European employment and in independent production. A comparison which would have to take account of the two aspects of both types of occupation, namely the proportion of cultivation intended for exchange and that intended for consumption.

Clearly the material for such a purpose does not exist in the incomplete, and sometimes exiguous, records of production for other than export purposes that issue from official sources. And even in regard to export crops, the actual area cultivated by peasants is rarely known. In the absence, therefore, of a productivity basis of comparison, we are left to estimate the position of European enterprise in the tropics in terms of the methods of organization of native economy which we have just discussed. And the indication of this appears to be that, without direct Governmental support, systems of production which rely on simple wage labour are declining relatively to those which use labour on some co-operative basis of free contract. The native is gradually increasing his possession of capital, either individually or co-operatively; but even where his position is entirely that of a cultivator supplying foreign-owned factories, a contract based on final prices gives him an interest in the entire process of production, and makes him to some extent participate in the risk—and the profits—of changes in the market demand for the finished product. The position of the European investor under these conditions depends less upon political privilege and more upon competitive function in the processes of production.

APPENDIX A

RELATIVE DENSITY OF POPULATION OF THE MAIN REGIONS[1]

[1] *I.Y.A.S.* for 1932. The ratios are derived from official records of the area and population of the respective countries for the date nearest 1931.

70·2 per square kilometre in Europe.
40·0 per square kilometre in Asia.
7·4 per square kilometre in North and Central America.
4·8 per square kilometre in Africa.
4·6 per square kilometre in South America.
1·2 per square kilometre in Oceania.

APPENDIX B

AREAS ALIENATED TO FOREIGN HOLDERS IN FREEHOLD OR LONG LEASEHOLD, AND AREAS RESERVED FOR NATIVE OCCUPANCY WHERE THE IMPERIAL GOVERNMENT HAS ASSUMED OWNERSHIP OF ALL LAND

TERRITORY	TOTAL AREA (SQUARE MILES)	ALIENATED (ACRES)	RESERVED (ACRES)
BELGIAN CONGO.. ..	920,000	3,718,440 (hectares)	—
FRENCH WEST AFRICA ..	1,604,000	147,193 (hectares)	—
KENYA	225,000*	7,750,000	106,000,000
MOZAMBIQUE	426,000	52,056† (square miles)	—
NYASALAND	48,000	4,000,300	—
NORTHERN RHODESIA ..	279,000	12,000,000	—
SOUTHERN RHODESIA ..	150,340	32,000,000‡	21,411,157 in perpetuity, 7,000,000 for sale to natives only
TANGANYIKA	373,490	2,000,000 (776,668 freehold)	—
UGANDA	94,204	6,394,141 to natives, 108,000 to Europeans, 27,000 to Indians	—

* Of which only 40,000 miles are estimated to be suitable for cultivation and 30,000 for grazing.

† The Territory administered by the Mozambique Company under charter. In 1929 the Government resumed the 73,500 square miles held by the Niassa Company. There are besides several smaller concessions for which figures do not appear to be published.

‡ With a further 3,500,000 acres in process of alienation in 1931. This land is chiefly for farming, while that in Northern Rhodesia is mainly for mining.

APPENDIX B—*continued*

TERRITORY	TOTAL AREA (SQUARE MILES)	ALIENATED (ACRES)	RESERVED
CEYLON	25,330	2,196,788*	—
FEDERATED MALAY STATES	27,430	2,829,450*	—
STRAITS SETTLEMENTS ..	1,531	725,000*	—
FIJI	7,000	532,605 freehold, 305,869 leased from natives	—
NETHERLANDS INDIES—			
Java and Madura ..	51,000	987,000 (hectares)†	—
Outer Provinces ..	204,000	1,608,773 (hectares)	—
NEW GUINEA .. .. (Mandated Territory)	93,000	272,375 (hectares)	—
PAPUA	90,540	245,500 700,000 vacant Crown lands	—

* In all these territories there are several small and large holdings which are non-European. In Ceylon they are held predominantly by Singalese, in Malaya by Chinese. These figures do not include the area which the Government regarded as being in effective native occupation when it assumed jurisdiction.

† From the *I.Y.A.S.* This figure does not include the short leases from natives under the law that foreign leases of native land must not amount to more than eighteen months in three years.

BIBLIOGRAPHY

I. DESCRIPTIVE AND HISTORICAL

ANSTEY, V. The Economic Development of India.

ANGOULVANT, G. Les Indes Neerlandaises.

BELL, SIR H. Foreign Colonial Administration in the Far East.

BEER, G. L. African Questions at the Peace Conference.

BÜCHER, K. Industrial Evolution.

BUELL, R. L. Native Policy in Africa. 2 volumes.

BUXTON, L. D. H. Primitive Labour.

CAMPBELL, P. Chinese Coolie Migration to Places within the British Empire.

DAY, C. The Dutch in Java.

DAVIS, M. (Editor). Modern Industry and the African.

DE KAT ANGELINO, A. D. A. Colonial Policy. 2 volumes.

DRIBERG, J. H. At Home with the Savage.

EDGERTON, H. E. Development of British Colonial Policy.

British Colonial Policy in the Twentieth Century.

ENOCH, C. R. The Tropics.

FAYLE, C. E. Short History of the World's Shipping Industry.

FIRTH, R. Primitive Economics of the New Zealand Maori.

FOSTER, SIR W. England's Quest of Eastern Trade.

FRANCK, L. (Éditeur). Études de Colonisation Comparée.

HARING, C. H. Trade and Navigation between Spain and the Indies.

HARMAND, J. Domination et Colonisation.

HOBHOUSE, GINSBERG, etc. Material Culture of the Simpler Peoples.

HUNTINGTON, E. The Human Habitat.

IRELAND, I. Tropical Colonisation.

The Far Eastern Tropics.

KEESING, F. M. Modern Samoa.

KELLER, A. G. Colonisation.

KNOWLES L. Economic Development of the Overseas Empire. Vol. I.
LUGARD. The Dual Mandate in British Tropical Africa.
MAANEN-HELMER, E. The Mandates System.
MACNAIR, H. F. The Chinese Abroad.
MCPHEE, A. Economic Revolution in British West Africa.
MAIR, L. P. An African People in the Twentieth Century.
MALINOWSKI, B. Argonauts of the Western Pacific.
MERCIER, G. Le Travail Obligatoire dans les Colonies Africaines. 1933.
MERIGNHAC, A. Traité de Legislation et d'Economie Coloniales.
MOON, T. P. Imperialism and World Politics.
MURRAY, SIR H. Papua To-day.
ORDE BROWNE, J. Vanishing Tribes of Kenya. 1925.
The African Labourer. 1933.
OLIVIER. White Capital and Coloured Labour.
The Pioneer Fringe. Edited I. Bowman. Published by the American Geographical Society.
ROBERTS S. H. Population Problems of the Pacific. 1927.
French Colonial Policy. 2 volumes, 1929.
SALZMAN, L. F. English Trade in the Middle Ages.
SARRAUT, A. La Mise en Valeur des Colonies Françaises.
SCHMIDT, M. Primitive Races.
SCHNEE, H. German Colonial Policy Past and Future. 1930.
SNOW, A. H. Aborigines in the Law and Practice of Nations.
SOUTHWORTH, C. The French Colonial Venture.
TAWNEY, R. H. Land and Labour in China.
THURNWALD, R. Economics in Primitive Communities.
TOWNSHEND, M. E. Rise and Fall of Germany's Colonial Empire.
WESTERMANN, D. The African To-day. 1934.

BIBLIOTHÈQUE COLONIALE INTERNATIONALE

Extension Intensive et Rationnelle des Cultures Indigènes. 1929.
Le Régime et l'Organisation du Travail des Indigènes dans les Colonies Tropicales. 1929.

2. AGRICULTURAL AND TECHNICAL

BUECHEL, F. A. Commerce of Agriculture.

DUDGEON, G. C. Agricultural and Forest Products of British West Africa.

FAULKNER and MACKIE. West African Agriculture.

JONES, C. F. South America. An Economic Geography.

LEAKE, H. M. Land Tenure and Agricultural Production in the Tropics.

PRUDHOMME, F. Plantes Utiles des Pays Chauds.

VANSTONE, J. H. Raw Materials of Commerce. Vol. II. Animal, Vegetable, Synthetic.

WATT, SIR G. Commercial Products of India.

WILCOX, E. W. Tropical Agriculture.

WILLIS, J. H. Agriculture in the Tropics.

The Banana. C. Fawcett.

The Banana in Caribbean Trade. J. T. Palmer, Economic Geography, July 1932.

Cacao, World Production and Trade. E.M.B., No. 27.

Coconut Palm Products. E.M.B., No. 61.

Coffee Growing. J. H. McDonald.

Copra and Coconut Oil. K. Snodgrass.

Cotton. Report on Cotton-Growing in Uganda, Kenya, and the Mwanza District of Tanganyika. C. N. French.

The Cotton-Growing Industry in Nigeria. C. N. French.

British Colonial Competition for the American Cotton Belt. L. Bader, Economic Geography, 1927.

Oil Palm Products. E.M.B., No. 54.

Oil Palm Industry in British West Africa. F. M. Dyke.

Oil Palm in Malaya. Bulletin of the Department of Agriculture. 1932.

Rice. Bulletin of the International Institute of Agriculture. March 1933.

Rubber. London and Cambridge Economic Service. Memorandum No. 34.

Bulletin of the Rubber Growers' Association. Monthly.

Sisal. E.M.B., No. 64.

Spices and Condiments. H. S. Redgrove.

Sugar. Economic Aspects of Sugar Cane Production. F. Maxwell.

Sugar: Report to the Economic Committee of the League of Nations. 1929. C. 148, M. 57.

Imperial Sugar Cane Research Conference, London, 1931. Report of Proceedings.

Tea, The Culture and Marketing of. C. F. Harler.

Tobacco. Vol. V, British Empire Survey, 1924.

Manufacturing Industries of the British Empire Overseas. Erlanger's. 1931.

Plantation Crops. E.M.B., C/5.

The International Yearbook of Agricultural Statistics.

An "Economic Commentary" on the Yearbook: The Agricultural Situation in 1929–30, and in 1930–31.

World Agriculture: A Survey. Royal Institute of International Affairs. 1932.

INDEX

For Product Safety Concerns and Information please contact our EU representative GPSR@taylorandfrancis.com Taylor & Francis Verlag GmbH, Kaufingerstraße 24, 80331 München, Germany